Darcy Millar was born and educated in London. After travelling in Australia, New Zealand and south-east Asia, he studied English literature at Manchester University. A student exchange took him to Copenhagen University for six months, where he discovered the delights of Scandinavian city life and resolved to make a career as an urbanist, specialising in cycle-friendly planning. While studying for master's degrees in Copenhagen and Malmö, he supported himself by working in a succession of cafés, steadily building his skills and developing a passion for all things coffee. Soon after graduating, he realised that office life was not for him, that he much preferred the buzz of service in a café. He began thinking about setting up his own business, on a modest scale at first – perhaps just a coffee cart. Fast-forward a few years, and he is living that dream as the proprietor of Darcy's Kaffe in Copenhagen, with two branches, eighteen staff and hundreds (perhaps even thousands) of regular customers, whom he regards as friends.

THE INSTANT COFFEE SHOP

HOW TO OPEN A CAFÉ IN A WEEK

DARCY MILLAR
WITH BRUCE MILLAR

HS
HEAD START

First published in 2023 by Palazzo Editions Ltd
15 Church Road
London SW13 9HE
www.palazzoeditions.com

Paperback ISBN 9781786751287
eBook ISBN 9781786751591

A CIP catalogue record for this book is available from the British Library.

Design and typesetting by Danny Lyle.

Printed in the UK
10 9 8 7 6 5 4 3 2 1

PROLOGUE

Every day, somebody somewhere opens a coffee shop. In the space of a few years, what was once a comparative rarity has become a standard feature on high streets and back streets around the world, bringing a fairly uniform set of drinks and a sense of community to millions of customers.

Many of the people setting up these coffee shops have never opened one before, and have never run their own business. I was one of them five years ago, when I dived in at the deep end and opened Darcy's Kaffe in Copenhagen. I took advice and guidance from wherever I could find it: from the internet, of course, and from many helpful individuals in the industry, to whom I owe profound thanks.

I also consulted plenty of books about coffee, but I scoured bookshops in vain for what I really wanted: a book about setting up your first coffee shop. So this is it – or at least my version. It is not a formula and does not pretend to be in any way definitive. Rather, it offers a range of guidance, advice and experience, tried and tested in a competitive marketplace and, thus far at least, successful to the extent that I now have two busy coffee shops and a bakery, operated by more than 20 staff.

If you read this book and absorb its contents, once you have secured a site and stocked up with the minimum necessary equipment and some coffee beans, you should be able to serve your first cup of coffee within seven days.

This is not to suggest it will be easy. It may even be the hardest-working week of your life. But it is doable. I know, because I have done it – three times.

Beyond that, you can improve your offer every day for the next thousand weeks.

CONTENTS

1 THE MODERN COFFEE SHOP

A global phenomenon; the 'third space';
changing social patterns; the decline of
alcohol; working and shopping from home;
a fantasy escape; waves of coffee.

So you want to open a coffee shop? Welcome aboard! Opening Darcy's
Kaffe in Copenhagen almost five years ago in late 2018 was a leap in the
dark for me, but it turned out to be the best decision I have ever made.

Before we get to the nuts and bolts of how to go about opening your
own, I think it is worth examining the position the coffee shop holds in
our culture, and the extraordinary proliferation of coffee shops around
the world in the past two decades. The contemporary coffee shop, selling
a globally recognised menu of coffee drinks – espresso, latte, flat white,
cappuccino, Americano – has become ubiquitous across great swathes
of the world. If the opening years of the 21st century will most likely
be remembered as the Digital Age, it could equally be called the Age of
the Coffee Shop – the two have expanded almost in tandem, and with
much the same customer base. This convergence has prompted one coffee
company to make the advertising boast: 'We've been serving flat whites
across London since before you could Instagram them.' (For the record,
like much of advertising it is not actually true: Instagram was launched
in 2010 and the company in question, which shall remain nameless, was
founded a year later, in 2011.)

This modern coffee shop is very much a global phenomenon, with
various geographical locations contributing to the overall picture. Early
inspiration, of course, came from Italy, the world leader in coffee mechani-
sation and consumption for much of the 20th century. Seattle, in the
American northwest, launched the behemoth of the genre, Starbucks, but
was also the birthplace of the mobile coffee cart – the ultimate expression
of the small-scale independent. Australia and New Zealand contributed
a laid-back Antipodean take on luxury, influenced by the large Italian
populations of Melbourne and Sydney, while Japan chipped in its intense
focus on artisan skills along with a minimalist aesthetic, and Scandinavia

added its concepts of the *fika* (coffee break) and *hygge* – both important to the atmosphere of coffee shops.

In many parts of the world, this new style of coffee shop has had to elbow its way into a marketplace that already has a well-established café scene. Paris and Vienna are prime examples, while Italy in particular, already home to tens of thousands of espresso bars, has witnessed some push-back against the new-fangled. A coffee shop in Florence was fined €1,000 in 2022 after charging a customer €2 for a decaffeinated espresso, on possibly trumped-up grounds that the price was not displayed on a menu behind the counter. Francesco Sanapo, the owner of Ditta Artigianale, insisted his was the 'first Italian coffee bar dedicated to quality coffee'; he had sourced the coffee in question from a small plantation in Mexico and his baristas had prepared it 'with great care', but a customer had taken offence at the price in a country where the standard espresso costs half that.

This modern style of coffee shop is not restricted to wealthy countries. In emerging economies you are of course most likely to find them in developed urban areas – I am pretty confident that I could land at an airport just about anywhere and order a flat white or an espresso within half an hour, quite possibly within the airport itself. But as long ago as 2003 the *New York Times* reported that in Egypt, where the basic breakfast of *ful medames* (stewed fava beans) is pretty much unchanged since the era of the pharaohs and where there's a long tradition of cafés serving tea, outfits selling lattes sprinkled with chocolate were springing up all over the place.

Given this proliferation, some might worry that we have reached saturation point: does the world really need another coffee shop? Well, my answer to this question is, yes, it certainly does.

In fact, I think we are only halfway through an enormous shift in taste and behaviour, whose multiple causes I will examine in this chapter. There will be booms and busts along the way. In the late 1980s, there were more than 200 coffee carts on the streets of Seattle alone – a bubble that duly burst. And as of early 2023, nobody who lives nearby can quite believe that the 23 coffee shops, of various types, on either side of a 300-metre stretch of London's South Circular Road in the southwest suburb of East Sheen (to take just one example) can all be financially sustainable. Perhaps they don't need to be. People open coffee shops for various reasons, not just to make money: it might be their passion project, or they've quit a high-pressure career with a good pay-off and want to work for themselves for a change, or they just fancy giving it a go. So yes, some of the 23 will probably not be there in two or five or ten years from now. But that does not mean there is no room for a new coffee shop in your neighbourhood, town or village.

THE BIG SHIFT

I believe that for various reasons there is a renewed demand for the 'third space' – a term coined by the sociologist Ray Oldenburg, home being the first space, the factory or office the second. Traditional examples of the third space include the market square, library, place of worship, barbershop, social club and pub – all of which have receded in importance in recent times. Communal activities such as shopping or going out to be entertained have retreated in the face of home deliveries and Netflix, while traditional work patterns have been undermined by the casualisation of employment and the growth of freelancing and 'wfh' (working from home).

But people are sociable beings; we need communal places to meet up and a home-from-home to relax in. The coffee shop now functions almost as a public service, occupying territory somewhere between the office on one hand and the bar or restaurant on the other. It can be a pit stop for refuelling and a hub for mobile workers, so it has a practical and functional purpose, but it is also somewhere to take a break from work or to hang out socially. This means it mixes practical, puritan appeal (inexpensive, part of the working day, alcohol-free) with self-indulgence (the rewarding 'little luxury' of delicious coffee and a slice of cake) – with none of the let-your-hair-down atmosphere of a bar serving alcohol, or the expense, formality and pressure to eat of a restaurant.

The culture around work has also changed. When my parents started working in the 1970s and 1980s, an office drinking culture was rife – and was often led by their line managers and bosses, who regarded time spent in bars as an essential if informal part of the induction and training process for anybody entering a new career. These days, employers are less tolerant of alcohol consumption during the lunch hour and most managers or senior executives would think twice before fraternising over a few drinks with younger staffers.

There is also an increasingly wide mix of genders and cultures in the workplace, so colleagues are less likely to head to a bar together outside office hours – but teams still need to unwind together away from the office. As for the increasing numbers of freelancers and employees working remotely, they still need a break from routine and possibly crave human company – hence the demand for coffee shops in residential areas.

The neutrality of the coffee shop – neither work nor home nor out-and-out entertainment venue – extends to its informal egalitarianism. Everybody is welcome, not just the millennials who constitute its core demographic. It is a safe public space, equally appealing to men and women. A lone woman will feel comfortable here – as will lone men, who can feel wary of entering a bar in case it functions as an informal clubhouse for the local hardmen. A mother will feel comfortable dropping in for a coffee and a snack with kids of any age in tow. And while few people would go to a coffee shop looking for romance or simply 'on the pull', a prospective couple can find it a good place to chat and get to know each other properly, without the pressures and expectations of a date in a bar or restaurant.

ALCOHOL IN RETREAT

Possibly the biggest single driver of the spread of coffee shops is the historic move away from alcohol as the social lubricant of choice. First of all, let me make it clear that I like decent beer, good wine and interesting cocktails far too much to play the puritan on this issue, and I have no real ethical qualms about serving alcohol to guests in the right context. But it is an unavoidable truth that overindulgence in alcohol can be extremely damaging to your health – and that increasing numbers of people across much of the world, especially younger people, are turning their backs on booze.

This shift away from alcohol consumption is led, as these global trends often are, by young people in rich countries. Levels of drinking have risen and fallen for various reasons throughout history, and there is not one single reason for the current decline. Health concerns seem to be part of the explanation, along with worries about the future, changes in technology and leisure activities, and changing relationships within families. As with all big trends, there is also an element of imitation, of fitting in: if people around you are drinking less, you tend to drink less yourself.

Dr Amy Pennay, a senior research fellow at La Trobe University's Centre for Alcohol Policy in Melbourne, monitors global drinking patterns. She says adolescent alcohol consumption has been in decline since the turn of the millennium: 'The US was the first place to peak, back in 1999. In Iceland, Sweden and Scandinavia the reduction started in 2001. Western

Europe, Canada, Australia and New Zealand followed, before most of Europe by the mid-2000s caught up.' So the process started a generation ago, and the cohort of young people who led the way in reduced drinking are now adults in their thirties.

In the UK, the proportion of late teenagers drinking alcohol every month dropped from 67 to 41 per cent between 2002 and 2019. The term 'sober curious' became current, indicating that even regular drinkers were considering abstinence, and in early 2023, one in six UK adults reportedly participated in 'dry January'.

Naturally, if people are drinking less, this means less trade for pubs and bars. The figures for the industry are stark: according to the pro-beer British lobby group CAMRA, three pubs closed down in the UK *every day* between July and December 2022. James Arkell, the chairman of Arkell's, a traditional family-owned brewery in the southwest England town of Swindon, put it bluntly: 'The small turnover pubs that had a regular ale-drinking customer base (seven days a week) have all but disappeared in that historic form.' The pubs that survive and even thrive may still look like pubs and still have traditional names on their signs – the King's Head, the Rose and Crown and so on – but in truth, they have morphed into restaurants. Overall, British pubs have made more money from food than from drink sales since 2010.

In France, a similar societal trend has had very different consequences for the drinks industry. Wine drinking per capita is down by two-thirds in the past 60 years, and half that decline has been in the past 10 years, driven by the 18 to 35 age group. Red wine has suffered the greatest losses, and the producers of Bordeaux have demanded government pay-outs to destroy vines and pour wine away in order to protect prices and liveli-hoods. According to French analysis, factors behind the downturn in alcohol drinking include lower consumption of red meat; fewer traditional family meals around a table, at which wine was de rigueur; and a rise in the number of single parents who don't want to drink alone.

If people are drinking less alcohol, that certainly does not mean they are going to abandon socialising – and if they are socialising, they will often do so over something to drink and a bite to eat. So coffee shops are moving into the territory abandoned by pubs and bars. In Britain, the figures for coffee shop openings more or less mirror those for pub closures, meaning that for every pub that closes, a coffee shop opens. The number of coffee shops is projected to overtake the number of pubs by 2030.

DEATH OF THE HIGH STREET

It's not just pubs and bars that are disappearing. There's another revolution in consumption patterns going on: the advent of shopping from home via the internet and delivery services.

As a result, Britain's Centre for Retail Research reports that an average of 47 shops closed down in the UK *every day* in 2022. The total of 17,145 closures was a 50 per cent increase on the previous year; 5,500 actually went bust, while the rest were either independent operators taking early retirement or bigger retailers 'rationalising' their branch networks.

This change is transforming the landscape in high streets, with empty shops multiplying, shopping parades disfigured by boarded-up facades, and both landlords and municipal authorities scratching their heads to find a solution.

One of the better ways of bringing life and footfall back to these streets, still the heart of their communities, is to facilitate the opening of independent coffee shops. Smart landlords and councils recognise that they can do their bit by making reasonable concessions on rent and rates, and removing the onerous deposits that deter start-ups – but they may need to be nudged in the right direction!

This vast new market for coffee does not, however, necessarily translate into easy pickings for independent coffee shops. The big chains have the resources to snap up the best sites, and made much of the running during the boom decades of 2000–2020. In a neat illustration of the transition from booze to coffee, Britain's biggest chain, Costa, was in fact owned through this period by Whitbread, historically the world's biggest brewer, but no longer brewing any beer at all. (In 2019 Whitbread sold Costa to Coca-Cola for £3.9 billion.)

New York and London in particular have also seen the growth of micro-chains founded by coffee fans with a private equity background; like tech start-ups, these rely on investors with deep pockets whose prime aim is to secure market share, with no urgent requirement to record a profit – hence the apparently cool 'independents' channelling an 'indie vibe', which can suddenly have half a dozen branches in prime locations within a year or two of launching. It may be difficult to compete with these guys, but their eagerness to grab a slice of the action shows how potentially lucrative the market remains.

However fierce the competition, I believe there is still room for the independent operator who provides real quality in whatever they offer, and who will respond quicker and better to the needs of the customer than either a franchisee or a manager working for investors. In the 10 years to 2020, the number of chain coffee outlets in London grew by 57 per cent to 2,195; in the same period, independents grew by 400 per cent, even though their overall number – growing to 400 – was much lower. There is also plenty of potential far away from metropolitan centres: one of the most interesting and progressive independents to emerge in Britain in recent years has been Bear, based in Uttoxeter, a market town in England's West Midlands best known for its racecourse.

WHY OPEN A COFFEE SHOP?

'It might be rash to leave a steady job to open up your dream café if you've got a big mortgage to repay.'

In his 2017 book *Carpe Diem Regained*, the popular philosopher Roman Krznaric needed to summon up a contemporary office worker's fantasy escape from the drudgery of their job.

He's certainly correct in his warning that the income of coffee shop owners may not meet your requirements, but what interests me is his choice of a typical escape fantasy. I think he is onto something: opening a café is something that many people dream of these days, and I suspect it is a relatively recent dream, one that people did not share 20 or 30 years ago.

So what is it that attracts somebody to open a coffee shop?

Given that it is a dream I had myself, and converted into reality, I think I know some of the answers. As Krznaric implies, opening your own coffee shop does indeed represent an escape from the drudgery of office life (although it can be hard work). You have no boss and you're not a tiny cog in a vast, impersonal machine. It is also the case that the barriers to launching into the trade are insignificant by comparison with the costs and skills required to launch almost any other hospitality business, whether a bar, hotel, pub or restaurant.

Start-up costs are tiny. Investment in premises, equipment, experience, training and staffing can all be minimal – there's no need for highly trained staff with various specialities (chef, pastry chef, sommelier, front of house and so on), for expensive kitchens with ventilation and extractors, for fancy crockery, cutlery, décor and furniture. Whatever your market, the licensing will be easier than any business involving the sale of alcohol or cooked food – and you won't have the problem of dealing with drunk customers.

This really is a business you can start as a one-person operation with a single coffee-making machine from a hole in a wall or mobile cart. Once you have that single machine, you can add extras at pretty minimal expense: a selection of fresh pastries that you can buy in from a supplier; sandwiches and cakes you may want to prepare yourself.

Enthusiasm, a willingness to learn and a real love of coffee will take you a long way. It also helps if you are interested in other people and take satisfaction from pleasing guests.

By hospitality industry standards at least, the working hours are attractive. You might have to get up a little earlier than many to be open by 7.30 a.m. or 8 a.m. in time to catch the breakfast/pre-work trade but in most cases you won't have to work late every evening.

Another attraction is the almost infinite flexibility of the coffee shop. We all know roughly what we expect to find at the bar: espresso-and-milk-based drinks, probably some snacks, but beyond that there really is no set style and you can combine coffee with almost any other interest – not just culinary. It is easy to hybridise, so there are coffee shops that also sell vinyl records and coffee bars tucked away inside surf shops or bicycle repair outfits, bookshops, galleries and museums. There were the internet cafés of the pre-mobile-device era, and today's gaming cafés. In a small village in southeast Sicily, I came across a young couple making ambitious modern coffee at a bar in front of a sit-down restaurant with a full burger menu featuring rare-breed local meat and indigenous vegetables; by night it morphed into a cocktail bar with the barista now mixing drinks.

THE RISE OF THE COFFEE CONNOISSEUR

We know that coffee is an affordable luxury for vast numbers of people. A small but growing proportion of these coffee drinkers are more discerning, and have developed a fine-tuned appreciation of the extraordinary variation of flavours, aromas and even textures available from a cup of coffee. These constitute a new breed of coffee connoisseurs, who beat a path to the high-quality coffee shops that offer them the chance to taste high-quality coffee from beans of specified provenance, roasted in small batches and possibly only available for a week or two.

These connoisseurs will think nothing of crossing town to taste a particular brew, and at weekends or on city-break trips they will put together itineraries taking in half a dozen or more independent coffee shops where they know they will taste something special. There is a coffee shop in Paris, Substance, where the barista-owner will guide customers *kaiseki*-style through a succession of cups over three hours, at a cost of €40 (£35) or so – but in fact, tasting rare and special coffees need not be prohibitively expensive, certainly by comparison to the oligarch-friendly prices of fine dining, fine wines or rare whiskies (even tea can get pricey to drink at the connoisseur level, as well as being difficult to find outside the Far East).

For all the spluttering over the high cost of a cup of coffee from an older generation who still hark after the €1 espresso, the market determines that there is a pretty standard price for a latte (to take just one example) in each locality. At the time of writing, a latte in London costs about £3.30 – you can expect to pay this in a chain outlet, and the same in a really ambitious independent coffee shop where the whole experience, including the flavour of the coffee, will be noticeably superior. So the independent is already looking like a bargain.

But what is truly remarkable is how easily you can trade up to drinking something very special. At a tiny independent specialist called Nostos, tucked away in the shadow of a railway bridge in Battersea, south London, on an ordinary weekday in February 2023 I could choose between a £3.30 latte; a 'standard' pour-over from Manhattan Coffee Roasters at £4.50; a 'rare' El Diviso from Colombia, roasted in-house, at £5.50; or a 'competition' Colombian geisha roasted by Meron Coffee of Transylvania at £7. So the very top of the range – a rarity imported from a surprising and exotic location – costs about twice the price of a standard milk-based coffee.

If you consider that £7 is a lot to spend on a cup of coffee, try trading up with a wine purchase and see where the price leads you. In London, I can pop into my local supermarket and pick up a bottle of plonk approximating to Bordeaux for perhaps £7.50. If I cross the road to the old-school wine merchant opposite and ask for a proper Bordeaux from a decent vintage, I'm likely to be shown a bottle costing 10 times as much, or even more: it could be £75, and will probably be well in excess of £100 if I've actually heard of the chateau.

This is part of the magic of the coffee shop: it can offer a stellar experience – the equivalent of a First Growth wine or a Michelin star meal – for little more than the bog-standard supermarket equivalent. Every day in Darcy's Kaffe we serve connoisseurs who recognise this – amateurs in the old sense, who enjoy training their palate to appreciate the range of flavours that coffee can offer, and who can afford to taste the best. For my generation, being a wine connoisseur is out of the question – few of us can even dream of drinking the famous stuff. With coffee, there's pretty much no limit to accessible quality.

2 HOW COFFEE CHANGED THE WORLD

Discovery and spread of coffee; influence of coffee shops on civilisation, politics and the arts; Italy's key role in coffee history; health drink and psychoactive drug of choice.

Back in my formative years, before I fell into the world of coffee shops, I studied history and English literature at school and university. So it's no surprise, perhaps, that when I began to immerse myself in all things coffee, looking at its role in culture and history became part and parcel of my newfound enthusiasm. And it's a fascinating history, too – one that I believe should interest anybody who works in the industry. So please bear with me while I share an overview of what I have learnt (if you're just bursting to find out how to open your own coffee shop, you may want to skip this chapter now and come back to read it later, once you're in business and have the odd quiet moment between slinging espressos).

Coffee – and the coffee shop – has of course been with us for several hundred years, if in rather different forms. But from the beginning, it has always been a progressive phenomenon, a mark of incipient modernity. We recognise this instinctively, even those of us who think we know nothing of the history of food and drink. Picture a scene in a TV drama set in historical times: ancient Egyptians or Britons swigging beer, Romans pouring libations of wine, Chinese sipping tea – all quite believable, as well as being historically accurate. But imagine any of them with a cup of coffee and the spell is broken, our belief in the fiction instantly shattered – we know the scene must be either a terrible mistake or some sort of joke.

Our ancestors have been fermenting fruit juice to make alcohol for millennia – it is a naturally occurring process that we simply learnt how to control. They must have been brewing infusions of leaves, herbs and flowers ever since they discovered how to bring containers of water to the boil – it was simply a matter of time before they settled on the leaves of the shrub *Camellia sinensis*, fermented, dried or toasted in various ways, as the primary but not the only 'tea' to drink. Other hot drinks have also been prepared since well before recorded history: savoury broths, warmed up or mulled versions of various alcoholic beverages, even chocolate (fermented as a drink by Mesoamericans more than 3,000 years ago and, like tea, exported onto global markets with the advent of long-distance sea trade).

Nobody is sure quite when coffee made its first appearance but it is certainly a recent beverage by historical standards, arriving on the cusp of what historians call the Early Modern era, in the late 1400s. Beans of the *Coffea arabica* plant may have been chewed in its native Ethiopia as a stimulus to energy long before anybody drank it, but historians such as Zeina Klink-Hoppe of the British Museum have singled out one particular person as responsible for introducing the beverage to the world: a Sufi sheikh by the name of Ali bin 'Ume al-Shadhili. He apparently spent some time in Ethiopia before returning home to the Yemeni port of Al-Mokha (after which the 20th-century Moka coffee pot and drink are named) around the year 1500, where he entertained his Sufi companions in the Shadhiliyya order with a brew made from boiled coffee beans. The stimulus of the caffeine helped them ward off sleep during *dhikr*, meditative rituals requiring the recitation of God's names late into the night.

Over the next century this new drink spread along trade and pilgrimage routes across Arabia, North Africa and the Levant, spilling into the secular sphere to be enjoyed by ordinary members of the community. Coffee houses emerged as meeting places where people of different social origins and ethnic or religious affiliations could gather, challenging traditional norms. Muslim lawyers debated whether coffee was a permissible drink – was it intoxicating? – but the real concern seems to have been the threat it posed to the social order. The first coffee ban on record was declared in the holy city of Mecca in 1511, after the governor, Kha'ir Bek Al-Mi'mar, encountered a group of men engaged in what he suspected was a conspiratorial conversation while drinking coffee in the precincts of the mosque at evening prayers. Coffee was banned in Cairo in 1517 and 1526, in Aleppo in 1543 and Damascus in 1546. Enforced closures of coffee houses as places of immoral and inappropriate behaviour are recorded again in Mecca (1525–1526) and Cairo (1539), in the holy cities of Mecca, Medina and Jerusalem in 1565, and across the whole Ottoman Empire in 1631.

But since coffee does not contain alcohol it escaped being banned on religious grounds throughout the Muslim world, and by 1600 there were as many as 600 coffee houses in Istanbul alone. The German cultural historian Wolfgang Schivelbusch has argued that coffee 'seemed to be tailor-made for a culture that forbade alcohol consumption and gave birth to modern mathematics' – a reference to its properties as an intellectual stimulant. Eventually, the Ottoman authorities reached a lucrative accommodation on the issue. Instead of banning coffee, they switched to taxing both the beans and the premises where they were enjoyed, so by the 1650s coffee houses were flourishing throughout the empire under government regulation – with income flowing into the imperial treasury's coffers.

By this time, coffee had begun to spread into Christian Europe via Venice, which controlled European trade with the Middle East. It became the first European city to have a coffee house in 1615, with Marseilles following in 1644, and Vienna, Oxford and London in the next few years.

COFFEE, CAPITALISM AND REVOLUTION
Oxford's second coffee shop opened in 1654 in Queen's Lane, where it is still in business today. Its founder, a Jewish immigrant from Syria named Cirques Jobson, came up with the idea of attracting regular custom by combining coffee with the innovation of free news sheets for reading at a large communal table – these were literally pieces of paper with handwritten items of news: the printed newspaper did not yet exist. In the view of Professor John Sommerville, emeritus professor of English history at the University of Florida: 'One might date the birth of the modern world from this development.'

This extraordinary claim is taken up by Tim Wu, a Columbia University law professor, *New York Times* op-ed writer and authority on the media who has advised Presidents Obama and Biden on internet policy. In his essay *How the Humble Coffee House Birthed Modern Media and Society*, Professor Wu writes that it:

marked the birth of a habit, one that remains with us – that of 'taking the news'. It is that itch you feel, that need to know what happened next in one of the various public stories you are following. When that habit attached itself to the printed newspaper, it became possible to speak of a rudimentarily informed public of some size who were following public events – a matter hard to imagine without some cheap way of distributing newspapers and space to read them in. Here, centuries before public libraries or public education, was the coffee house, perhaps, outside of the ancient city square, the first truly public forum for the mass dissemination of information necessary to 'public opinion'.

In this way and others, the history of civilization would surely be different without the coffee house…

Today, the coffee house may no longer be the center of public news distribution, though it remains an important place for intellectual input and output. So the next time you find yourself in a café, with a coffee in hand, reading a newspaper, beginning to form an opinion, you might reflect that in this ritual you are, in a small way, contributing to a tradition that gives the word 'citizen' its deeper meaning, and makes democracy plausible.

The role of the coffee shop in the development of the modern world does not end here. In fact, it crops up Zelig-like as the setting for countless other turning points in European social, political, cultural, intellectual and economic history – whenever, it sometimes seems, sharp and original thinking was required.

Let's start in London, where the Great Fire of 1666 destroyed much of the civic infrastructure just as the city was becoming a centre for world trade. Merchants began meeting informally in the coffee houses that sprang up as the city was rebuilt, and by 1688 there were as many as 80 of them, each providing a meeting place for a specific trading interest. Among the most famous was Edward Lloyd's coffeehouse, on Tower Street near the River Thames, where ship owners and captains gathered to exchange information – and where they were soon joined by brokers wanting to sell them the insurance they needed to underwrite the dangerous but enormously profitable business of sending a ship off on a voyage that might take several years to the ends of the known world. In 1691 Lloyd's moved to new premises at 16 Lombard Street, and in 1734 it began publication of *Lloyd's List* to detail maritime information. This is now one of the world's longest-running publications, and Lloyd's remains the world's largest insurer of maritime trade – more important than ever in our age of globalisation.

A few minutes' walk away in Exchange Alley, two coffee shops attracted stockbrokers who had been banned from the official Royal Exchange

– business owners then, as now, preferred independence and self-regulation to government scrutiny and official rules. One of these shops, Garraway's, became the first place to sell tea imported from the Far East in 1657 and in 1671 it hosted the first sale of furs by the Hudson's Bay Company, opening up what became a massively lucrative trade with European markets. The most important coffee shop of all was Jonathan's, although it no longer operates under that name; established in 1680, it became a meeting place for brokers in stocks and shares, with stock prices posted on the wall from 1698. In 1761 a club of brokers transformed it into the London Stock Exchange, the world's biggest until it was overtaken by the New York Stock Exchange in 1919.

While the coffee houses of London may have ushered in the birth of modern capitalism, those of Paris had an equally profound effect in the realms of politics and culture. Possibly the first and certainly the most famous was Le Procope in Saint-Germain-des-Prés, founded in 1686 by Procopio Cutò, an energetic Sicilian who is also credited as the inventor of gelato. The next year, the Comédie-Française theatre happened to open across the road, guaranteeing the café a steady stream of Parisian movers and shakers. In the following century it hosted everyone from Queen Marie-Antoinette and Napoleon to the philosophers Rousseau and Voltaire (who was said to drink 40 cups of coffee mixed with chocolate a day, a feat of consumption later matched by Honoré de Balzac, who swallowed balls of ground coffee on an empty stomach to power his prodigious output of novels). Le Procope's habitués did not just gossip idly over their drinks: Voltaire's fellow philosopher Denis Diderot planned his great work, the *Encyclopédie*, at its tables, while Robespierre, Danton and Marat, who all lodged nearby, plotted the French Revolution here. They weren't Le Procope's only revolutionaries: the United States' founding fathers Benjamin Franklin and Thomas Jefferson were regulars during their ambassadorial stints to the court of Versailles.

During the 19th century, Paris became the world's most famous city of cafés, and by the early 1900s it boasted 10,000 of them. Many provided paper for their customers, who included intellectuals, artists and bohemians as well as straightlaced members of the bourgeoisie. Some of the most famous cafés in Paris date from this era: Café de la Rotonde in Montparnasse, near Picasso's studio, where Jean Cocteau, Modigliani, Diego Rivera and Peggy Guggenheim would hang out. On the Left Bank,

Les Deux Magots and Café Flore drew an all-star cast including Ernest Hemingway, Jean-Paul Sartre, Albert Camus and Edith Piaf.

Other European capitals developed distinctive café traditions, none more glorious than that of Vienna, which is now listed by Unesco as Intangible Cultural Heritage. Here, the tradition even cultivated a unique foundation myth – that the city's love affair with coffee originated with the discovery of beans left behind by the Ottoman Turks retreating after their failure to take Vienna in the great siege of 1683. Whether this really happened or not, Vienna's café culture developed in the following decades and spread to regional capitals throughout the Austro-Hungarian empire, from Prague and Budapest to Lviv and Milan.

Cultural figures who frequented Vienna's cafés ranged from the city's great composers of the classical and romantic eras – Mozart, Beethoven and Schubert – through to the artists and thinkers of the early 20th century: Gustav Klimt, Robert Musil, Sigmund Freud and the 'Vienna Circle' of logical positivist philosophers. A single Viennese *Kaffehaus*, the Café Central, can list Lenin, Stalin, Trotsky, Tito and Hitler among its customers – a truly imposing line-up of 20th-century titans, even if they never all turned up on the same day.

Stefan Zweig, the great Viennese chronicler of Mitteleuropa before the First World War, described the *Kaffehaus* scene of the 1890s, during his teenage years (and came to much the same conclusion as Professor Wu a century later):

the Viennese coffee house is an institution of a peculiar kind, not comparable to any other in the world. It is really a sort of democratic club, and anyone can join it for the price of a cheap cup of coffee. Every guest, in return for that small expenditure, can sit there for hours on end, talking, writing, playing cards, receiving post, and above all reading an unlimited number of newspapers and journals. A Viennese coffee house of the better sort took all the Viennese newspapers available, and not only those but the newspapers of the entire German Reich, as well as the French, British, Italian and American papers, and all the major literary and artistic international magazines, the *Mercure de France* as well as the *Neue Rundschau*, the *Studio*, and the *Burlington Magazine*. So we knew everything that was going on in the world at first hand, we heard about every book that came out, every theatrical performance wherever it took place, and we compared the reviews in all the newspapers. Perhaps nothing contributed so much to the intellectual mobility and international orientation of Austrians as the fact that they could inform themselves so extensively at the coffee house of all that was going on in the world, and at the same time could discuss it with a circle of friends. We sat there for hours every day, and nothing escaped us

(from *The World of Yesterday*, 1942, translated
from the German by Anthea Bell).

MODERN TIMES

The 20th century, the so-called 'People's Century', saw the transformation of coffee into a drink for the masses rather than just metropolitan sophisticates. This depended largely on a series of technological breakthroughs, beginning neatly in 1900 with the development of canned, vacuum-packed ground coffee by US company Hill Bros., which enabled ordinary grocery shops to stock fresh coffee to be brewed at home. Around the same time, the process for creating instant soluble coffee was invented and patented twice, by New Zealander David Strang and by Satori Kato, a Japanese chemist based in Chicago. Instant coffee has reigned supreme ever since in millions of homes and offices, and still accounts for more than three-quarters of the coffee consumed in British homes.

Fittingly it was Italy, the European country with the longest history of coffee drinking, that contributed most to the creation of modern coffee consumption – so much so that coffee now stands alongside pasta and pizza as global symbols of Italian taste. Hence the cod-Italian nomenclature of today's global coffee industry, some of which is baffling to actual Italians (my father once made the mistake of ordering a *latte* in Sicily; he was given a glass of hot milk, at 11 a.m.). Another invention from the turn of the century set the ball rolling – namely Luigi Bezzera's 1901 patent for a gas-heated brass boiler which produced steam to force water through a 'cake' of coffee. This new style of coffee became known as an 'espresso', with a triple play on the word: water was 'expressed' under pressure through the ground coffee; the cup was made 'expressly' for each customer; and it echoed the 'express' trains that epitomised speed and progress in the 'Age of Steam'.

This fast new style revolutionised coffee service, which had until then taken place at tables with waiters, much like tea shops or, for that matter, restaurants. American-style bars became fashionable, at which customers would stand for their shot of coffee served by a 'barista' (an Italianisation of the English 'barman'). Elaborate coffee machines with the Art Deco styling of the inter-war era adorned these bars, becoming part of the theatre of the coffee shop; such was demand that by the outbreak of war in 1939 there were 22 companies in Milan alone producing these machines.

Italians also wanted to drink real coffee at home, in preference to the instant varieties that prevailed elsewhere. In 1933 Alfonso Bialetti introduced the Moka pot – the stove-top percolator which is now seen in 90 per cent of Italian households. (His heavily moustachioed son Renato, who took over the firm in 1946, was the model for the company's cartoon emblem. When he died in 2016 at the age of 93, his ashes were interred in a replica Moka pot.)

THE ESPRESSO

A further engineering advance drove the popularity of the Italian espresso bar still higher in the post-war era. Milanese bar owner Achille Gaggia spent 10 years perfecting a method of eliminating the unpleasant burnt flavours of espresso coffee, and in 1947 registered a patent for a lever-operated piston with gearing and a spring that would force water from the boiler through the coffee cake under nine atmospheres of pressure – much higher than hitherto, but at a significantly lower temperature. The resultant espresso was brown instead of black, with essential oils and colloids creating a mousse or 'crema' on the surface. A former Gaggia employee, Ernesto Valente, provided the finishing touches to the technology with the Faema E61, introduced in 1961, which used an electric pump to draw water directly from the mains, pressurise it and pass it through a heat exchanger. This 'semi-automatic' machine is still the standard model in Italy.

So now the Italian coffee shop, or caffè, could offer a delicious drink that was impossible to replicate at home – launched to coincide with the Sixties' economic miracle, in which an increasingly affluent society saw a mass internal migration, mainly from the poorer south to new jobs in north Italian towns and cities. Here, people would meet up in caffès after work and at weekends to watch football on newly introduced television – hence the popularity of the name Caffè Sport. In 1956, Italy's 84,000 caffès were outnumbered by 93,000 traditional restaurants, trattorias and osterias. By 2001, caffè numbers had climbed steadily to 141,000, while the number of restaurants – despite half a century's growth in tourism – had dropped to 86,000.

Italian entrepreneurs were quick to see the export opportunities, with both Gaggia and Faema opening subsidiaries in Barcelona in the 1950s. In Germany, Italian ice cream parlours found coffee a useful alternative product to sell during their dead winter season. In Britain, wartime rationing was finally lifted in 1952 and the next year the first Gaggia espresso machine was installed at the Moka coffee bar in Frith Street, Soho (which was declared open by the Italian actress Gina Lollobrigida). It was a huge hit with young Londoners emerging from the era of post-war austerity and spawned numerous imitators. One of these, the 2i's around the corner in Old Compton Street, hosted the first performances of home-grown British rock'n'roll by Cliff Richard, Adam Faith and Joe Brown, and within a decade 'Swinging London' was the most happening city in the world.

Across the Atlantic in New York, the coffee bars of Greenwich Village played a similar role in the development of the new youth music scene. The Gaslight Café, opened in 1958, and the Caffe Reggio, which claimed to have served the first cappuccino in North America, hosted early performances from the young folkie Bob Dylan when he arrived in the city in 1961. He also played at Cafe Wha? (1959), where Jimi Hendrix, Bruce Springsteen and the Velvet Underground all made early appearances.

THE WAVES OF COFFEE

Industry insiders and analysts often speak of coffee world developments in terms of waves – as in 'Third Wave coffee'. It is worth knowing what these stand for, even if the definitions are far from precise.

First Wave:

The mass-market coffee scene of the 20th century, consisting mainly of filter coffee in the hospitality industry and instant coffee at home, with different approaches in local markets.

Second Wave:
The global spread of an espresso-based milk coffee culture in the 1990s, led by chains, most notably Starbucks.

Third Wave:
The rise of independent coffee shops in the early 2000s, with a focus on high-quality beans and artisan skills in roasting and making coffee.

As soon as the concept of the Third Wave was invented, a Fourth and Fifth were probably inevitable, although from here on the terminology becomes increasingly fanciful...

Fourth Wave:
Further refinement of coffee-making skills through the 2010s, with scientific focus on water quality, accurate measurement and micro-roasting, plus the addition of special ingredients such as non-dairy milk.

Fifth Wave:
A catch-all term that is used to denote anything new and avant-garde in the world of coffee.

While Italian-style espresso remained the basis of coffee served in espresso bars around the world, what non-Italians actually drank was domesticated for each market. In English-speaking countries, where American-style milk bars had been familiar since the 1930s, this meant serving a hybrid between coffee and milkshake, in the form of a cappuccino with frothy warm milk topped with powdered chocolate, served with plenty of brown sugar.

There were other developments too. Alfred Peet, who had been trained to roast by his coffee wholesaler father in his native Holland, established Peet's Coffee in Berkeley on San Francisco Bay in 1966, where he introduced high-quality arabica beans to the American West Coast. The Speciality Coffee Association of America was founded in 1982 to boost the sale of premium-quality beans, preferably from a single region or even estate. Originally this was marketed towards home consumers, but 'gourmet' retailers promoting their produce by making coffee in-store attracted a following with a version of a traditional café au lait under the Italian name of 'caffè latte', in which 'textured' (that is, steamed) milk is poured over a strong espresso base. The visual theatre of the preparation gained its final touch in the form of 'latte art' – the barista's signature design that proved that each cup was handmade and unique.

Seattle, on the northern edge of the West Coast, was at the forefront of this new breed of coffee shop in the 1980s, in tandem with the city's emergence as capital of the new computer-based economy – and, incidentally, spawning ground of rock music's new grunge scene. Microsoft had moved its headquarters to Seattle in 1979, and the next year a certain Chuck Beek opened Monorail Espresso, claimed to be the world's first guerrilla mobile coffee cart. By the end of the 1980s as many as 20 Seattle companies were building carts for sale across the US.

The city also nurtured Starbucks, originally a roastery modelled on Peet's which was reconceived by Howard Schultz as a coffee shop and became by a large margin the biggest name in the so-called 'Second Wave' of coffee that surged around the world from the 1990s – and made inroads into the traditional tea-drinking market of China in the early 2000s. Schultz, a billionaire several times over who has toyed with the idea of running for US president, finally stood down from Starbucks after three separate stints as chief executive, on 1 April 2023. He signed off with a final earnings call to analysts and investors in which he reaffirmed the Italian inspiration for the chain – and capped it with a mysterious promise of something new from the same source:

> It was 1983, walking the streets of Milan, and having the inspiration for what Starbucks could one day be. Now 40 years later, we have more than 36,000 stores around the world, serving in excess of 100 million customers each week.

> While I was in Italy last summer [2022], I discovered an enduring transformative new category and platform for the company – unlike anything I have experienced. The word I would use to describe it without giving too much away is alchemy. It will be a game-changer. So stand by.

We stood by, and a few weeks later Starbucks unveiled Schultz's 'transformative' new development: the 'oleato' – coffee served with a shot of extra virgin olive oil. Do American billionaires make April Fools jokes? Possibly not, but the announcement certainly generated millions of dollars' worth of publicity, with coverage in newspapers around the world. Which was presumably the main aim of the exercise.

COFFEE AND HEALTH
'It is excellent to prevent and cure the dropsy, gout and scurvy'

Pasqua Rosée, most likely a Greek from Ragusa in what is now Croatia, was hired as a local fixer in Smyrna, Turkey, by an English merchant working for the Levant Company, who helped him set up London's first coffee shop when the pair returned to England in 1652 – a stall on the edge of St Michael's churchyard off Cornhill. That year, he published a handbill entitled *The Vertue of the Coffee Drink*, proclaiming the new-fangled elixir as a cure for the era's most dreaded illnesses – 'dropsy' being the general term then for heart disease. It also, he said, offered protection against 'scrofula' (tuberculosis), miscarriages, 'spleen, hypocondriack winds and the like'.

This sounds very like the unscientific patter of snake-oil salesmen through the ages, and I am usually pretty wary of studies and statistics claiming that coffee is a specifically healthy drink, for a number of reasons. First of all, I am not a scientist or a statistician and I take the standard sceptical view that you can prove anything (and therefore nothing) by manipulating statistics. So I take the various claims and counter-claims related to health and diet with a big pinch of salt: good carbs vs bad carbs; salt vs sugar; butter kills vs fat is good (although I can't help but agree that fat is flavour).

Secondly, I don't really think that people drink coffee because it is healthy, but because it tastes delicious and is an enjoyable social beverage.

Thirdly, I am pretty sure that any active health benefit conferred by drinking coffee is dwarfed by the benefits of its role as an alternative to alcohol. There is no avoiding the fact that alcohol does tremendous harm to a great many people, partly through the social pressures of its being the default drink in so many public and private contexts. When I worked in a pub, it was immediately clear to me that a number of our 'best' clients – that is, regulars who dropped in most days for several drinks – were suffering from health problems as a direct consequence of their alcohol intake. I never get this impression from customers in a coffee shop.

Having made this disclaimer, it is certainly the case that a significant proportion of customers in today's cafés can be described as 'conscious' consumers – that is, they are aware of the ethical and health implications of what they eat and drink, and make choices accordingly. This is why most coffee shops now offer a wide range of non-dairy, gluten-free, vegan, vegetarian, organic and sugar-free options. So any coffee shop proprietor would do well to know a bit about the science.

One recent piece of research will be of interest to any customers seeking reassurance about coffee consumption on health grounds. Published on 27 September 2022 in the *European Journal of Preventive Cardiology*, a study conducted by Peter Kistler of the Baker Heart and Diabetes Research Institute in Melbourne, Australia, looked at the health records and coffee consumption of almost half a million people over more than 12 years. It found clear evidence that drinking two or three cups a day is linked with a longer lifespan and reduced risk of contracting heart disease. The figures are pretty startling: compared with those who did not drink coffee at all, drinkers of ground coffee were 27 per cent less likely to die from any cause; of decaffeinated coffee, 14 per cent less likely to die; and of instant coffee, 11 per cent less likely to die.

Professor Kistler and his colleagues adjusted the figures to account for the effects of other influences, ranging from the ethnicity and sex of the individuals to their other illnesses, their consumption of tea, and whether they smoked or drank alcohol. The figures for fatalities and cardiovascular disease indicate that all coffee drinkers gain a measure of protection from drinking coffee. In all cases, ground coffee was seen to confer the highest level of protection.

Perhaps even the allowances made by the research team do not fully take into account the advantages that the 82,000 participants who drank 'proper' ground coffee enjoy in life: they are likely to be richer, better educated and more conscious of what they eat and drink than other consumers – all factors that contribute to better health. But the sheer scale of the improved outcome in tens of thousands of lives cannot be ignored. In fact, Professor Kistler makes no attempt to pinpoint precisely how and why coffee promotes better health, and he is extremely modest in his claims for its benefits – which, to me, makes them all the more believable. He concludes:

Caffeine is the most well-known constituent in coffee, but the beverage contains more than 100 biologically active components. It is likely that the non-caffeinated compounds were responsible for the positive relationships observed between drinking coffee, cardiovascular disease and survival. Our findings indicate that drinking modest amounts of coffee of all types should not be discouraged but can be enjoyed as a heart-healthy behaviour.

Professor Kistler says nothing about drinking coffee in pregnancy, or about caffeine intolerance in general. So I would point out, first, that doctors advise pregnant women to confine their consumption to one cup of coffee a day, while both the US Department of Agriculture and the European Food Safety Authority recommend limiting overall daily caffeine intake to about 400 milligrams, between four and five cups of coffee or six to seven single-shot espressos.

As for individual caffeine intolerance, it makes sense for any coffee drinker who has trouble sleeping to limit their intake, especially later in the day, and even give it up for a while to see if it makes any difference. It is also the case that the amount of caffeine in a single cup of coffee varies enormously – even between cups brewed from the same beans in the same shop. The good news for customers of independent coffee shops is that the cheaper robusta beans used by many chains are much higher in caffeine than the high-quality arabica beans used by independents.

If you enjoy sport, multiple studies showing how consuming a cup of coffee an hour or so before exercise can boost alertness, mental focus, metabolism, energy and endurance levels have recently been cited in publications including the *Journal of the International Society of Sports Nutrition* and the *British Journal of Sports Medicine*. Coffee also aids recovery and reduces post-exercise muscle soreness – as is witnessed by the queues of tracksuit-wearing customers in any café close to a gym.

ALTERED STATES

In a brilliant analysis in his recent book *This Is Your Mind on Plants* (2022), the American food writer Michael Pollan points out that something like 90 per cent of humans ingest caffeine regularly, making it the most widely used psychoactive drug in the world, and the only one we routinely give to children (commonly in the form of soda). Few of us even think of it as a drug, much less our daily use of it as an addiction. It's so pervasive that it's easy to overlook the fact that to be caffeinated is not baseline consciousness but, in fact, an altered state. It just happens to be a state that virtually all of us share, rendering it invisible.

Pollan is talking, of course, about both coffee and tea drinkers – tea leaves in fact contain higher levels of caffeine than coffee beans, although the differing methods of extraction mean there is roughly twice as much caffeine in a cup of coffee as in a cup of tea.

He also points out that 1,3,7-trimethylxanthine, the scientific name for the caffeine molecule, makes its way swiftly into every molecule of the human body when it is consumed. And we humans are not the only addicts: bees will return to caffeinated flowers even though the nectar supplies have been depleted, which means they neglect foraging for fresh nectar that boosts honey production – worryingly junkie behaviour.

Strikingly, Pollan examines how caffeine – in the form of tea and coffee – helped drag Europeans out of the 'alcoholic fog' of the Middle Ages and enabled them to override the natural cycles of darkness and sleep. 'It's difficult to imagine an Industrial Revolution without it,' he writes, tracing the exploitation involved both in farming tea and coffee in the tropics and in dragging more work out of the caffeine-drugged workforce in Europe or North America. So this may be the darker side of the various historical transformations we have traced in these pages – the invention of capitalism, the development of newspapers, politics, avant-garde literature and art, the radical departures in philosophy and psychology, and the emergence of pop music.

It seems too late for us to return to a state of nature. There are too many of us on earth, and our complex societies require enormous feats of organisation – could we afford to, and would we want to, return to the alcoholic fog of the pre-caffeine era? Clearly there is a lot more that science needs to study. What are the 100 and more biological components that Professor Kistler refers to, and how exactly do they benefit our health?

But what we do know – what Professor Kistler has shown – is good enough for me as it stands; perhaps there was something in Pasqua Rosée's claims, after all. I for one am going to carry on drinking three or four cups of delicious real coffee a day – because I enjoy it, and I'm happy in the knowledge that it is doing me good.

3 HOW I FELL INTO THE COFFEE BUSINESS

First sips in London, Sydney and Raglan, New Zealand; Copenhagen calls; no taste for office life.

I was a late and reluctant coffee drinker. As a child I had narrow, utterly conventional tastes, preferring pizza or pasta to the home-cooked meals conjured up by my father. Even into my late teens, well after I had acquired a taste for beer or wine, I would never order a coffee when out and about, never drink one at home.

My first real experience of coffee came in the summer I left school, when I managed to get a holiday job in a café and, shockingly it now seems to me, was allowed – even encouraged – to make a drink I had never properly tasted. This was not a greasy-spoon joint serving mugs of Nescafé but a fashionable café in an historic former bishop's palace beside the Thames in Fulham, west London – the sort of upmarket place where staff would occasionally recognise a face from television or a supermodel.

The coffee came from a shiny stainless-steel machine that towered over the counter, hissing steam. Operating this big toy looked like fun, I thought, so when the opportunity came to have a go myself, I jumped at it – despite having no idea what was required of me. A colleague ran briefly through the options – espresso, cappuccino, latte and Americano – without actually showing me what to do, and I was away, essentially clueless: I really had no idea at all how to make a proper cup of coffee.

Oddly enough, I vividly remember one customer thanking me for making such a good coffee. I'm not going to stake a claim to possessing some prodigious natural talent as a barista, and nor do I think I fluked it. What I believe now is that, just a dozen years ago, coffee was simply not taken seriously. Making a cup of coffee was considered to be much the same as dunking a tea bag into a mug and pouring some boiling water over it. And this held true even at a professionally run café in a fashionable part of the British capital.

Attitudes have certainly changed – both mine, and those of a vast swathe of the general population. In my own coffee shop in Copenhagen, we recently gave a trial to an experienced chef and baker who wanted to try her hand as a barista. I noticed immediately that as she went about her work she was chewing gum – never a good look when you're serving customers. Worse still, she was still chomping away when she sipped and tasted the drink. How could she possibly pick up the nuances of flavour? Needless to say, she did not last in the role.

My experience at the bishop's palace failed to convert me into a coffee drinker, and the busy summer season soon came to an end. I still needed money to fund the trip to exotic lands that I had in mind before going to university, and there were other options in hospitality where I could earn it. In the space of a couple of months, I both scaled the heights and plumbed the depths.

Let's start at the bottom, with the few weeks I spent as a barman at what must have been the cheapest pub in west London (which I won't name in case the licensee is still active in the trade). The kitchen was a filthy mess that could only have passed hygiene inspections on an exchange of money, while at the bar a shot of spirits could be had for under £1. The regulars were a friendly enough bunch – it wasn't a threatening or violent place – but even in the younger ones, the effects of habitual drinking were depressingly obvious as they stumbled over their words and struggled to hold their end of a conversation. This was probably a very good lesson to learn for a teenage school-leaver just setting out on adult life. It was also an environment I was happy to escape as soon as I could.

At the other end of the scale, I managed to wangle my way into some shifts as a waiter at the River Café, a hugely successful if pleasingly informal operation a couple of hundred yards along the Thames from the bishop's palace, once described by the *New York Times* as the world's greatest Italian restaurant and now a Mecca that drew foodies from all over the world.

If my time there was short, it was also blissful. For a start, the entire staff sat down before service to sample their way through pretty much the whole menu. This was an incredible perk, given that the produce and the cuisine were world class. It set the front-of-house team up for the shift ahead, ensuring we were in a happy mood when we encountered guests. There was also a practical benefit: if we knew the dishes by taste, we would be in a much better position to answer tricky questions and give little nuggets of enthusiastic advice to customers who asked us – nothing is more frustrating for customers than a clueless and unhelpful waiter.

There were other ways in which the River Café ensured that staff really bought into its ethos and identified with its approach. We waiters would pick, clean and chop the herbs that garnished plates, which helped us feel part of the broader kitchen team, breaking down the barrier between front-of-house and kitchen staff.

But it must be said that I fell short as a waiter by the high standards required at such an elevated institution. To be frank, I couldn't even clear a table without breaking into a nervous sweat, which meant I was of little use in such a busy place – I was probably more of a hindrance than a help. My manager was very encouraging when she informed me that I would not be booked for any further shifts: I clearly had the right attitude, I was told, but I needed to gain more experience somewhere a little less frantic – after which I would be welcomed back with open arms.

So I left without any bitterness. And I can say now that I was certainly inspired by what I saw could be achieved in hospitality. The River Café was above all a place where simple food was presented perfectly, and where a casual and relaxed atmosphere was made possible by impeccably professional standards of service. This was another lesson for life – and an approach I aspire to every day in my own business.

AUSTRALIA, NEW ZEALAND AND A COFFEE REVELATION

A few months later found me in Sydney. The cost of my flight to Australia had pretty well exhausted my meagre savings, so once again I was looking for casual work. Cafés are eternally on the look-out for staff, and I duly pitched up for an audition at a promising-looking little independent, where the manager asked me to fix him a flat white while he watched.

Not surprisingly, the 'experience' back in the bishop's palace that I quoted on my résumé was less than rigorous, and had certainly not prepared me for this ordeal. The manager watched patiently as I struggled to grind the beans correctly, then tamp the grounds, steam the milk and pour. I failed pretty comprehensively to make the grade as a barista.

Luckily I managed to pick up a gig pedalling tourists better-heeled than me around the city centre in a Bangkok-style rickshaw. With the money I saved doing this for a few months, I flew on to New Zealand for a road trip by camper-van with a bunch of friends – and it was here, prompted by the need to stay alert while driving long distances, that I really discovered the joy of drinking coffee.

In fact, I can be still more specific. It was at a small surf resort called Raglan, about 100 miles south of Auckland on the North Island and famous for its black sand beach, that I experienced what I now realise was the life-changing, career-shaping revelation that coffee was something very special.

I even remember why we went to this particular coffee bar: we had picked up a map of the locality at a petrol station/tourism office, and it contained a voucher offering two coffees for the price of one at Raglan Roast. That bribe might not have been enough to sway me, but one member of our party had already picked up a caffeine habit and suggested that we give it a go. And the coffee? Full tasting but not at all bitter, the texture creamy and smooth (I had ordered a latte). It was the first time I had ever positively enjoyed a cup of coffee, and the moment has stayed with me. I ordered a second cup – perhaps even a third.

From then on, I'd stop off somewhere most days for a coffee and a slice of the ubiquitous banana bread. I soon discovered that just about every neighbourhood or town in Australia or New Zealand, no matter how small or out of the way it seemed, would have a little shop serving serious coffee.

THE 'THIRD WAVE' REACHES BRITAIN

If this was not yet the case in England a dozen years ago, things were beginning to stir. Soon after my return, I came across the Small Batch roastery near Hove station in Brighton, an early – and still thriving – example of the Third Wave independent coffee shops that have since proliferated across the country. It was here that I first saw a Hario syphon brewer in action, and was drawn into the extravagant theatricality that can accompany the serving of coffee – the suggestion of the mad scientist poring over phials, glass globes and Bunsen burners to produce wonderful flavours, just as Heston Blumenthal had done with cooking at his world-famous restaurant The Fat Duck. This, by the way, is not just a fanciful idea: the Japanese company Hario was founded more than 100 years ago to manufacture heatproof glassware for use in laboratories, and only turned to coffee-making equipment during the post-war consumer boom.

I bought a coffee guide book and as a student in Manchester I explored the coolest-looking cafés in the city – often satisfying myself with a snoop through the window from my bicycle seat, while I hoarded my cash for the occasional beer-swilling night out. When I did treat myself to a coffee, my choices were not what I now think of as serious or sophisticated. I never ordered a filter coffee or a good espresso, and like 80 per cent of customers I drank my coffee with frothy steamed milk. Then I would add my own touch: a thin layer of brown sugar through which I would sip the milky drink. I thought of it, I suppose, as a naughty treat – a dessert in a cup, a liquid panna cotta.

At some point, though, it dawned on me that I did not need to go to a café to enjoy a coffee – and I certainly could not afford to do so on a daily basis. Instead, I could buy a bag of ground beans for £4 and consume 10 to 15 cups, each costing pennies rather than pounds. The only equipment required for home brewing was a cheap plastic V60 (produced by Hario) and some filters – the basic components of the pour-over, one of the best methods to make coffee.

Around this time I also launched what I now recognise was my first foray as a hospitality entrepreneur. With a friend, I took orders from fellow students for filled bagels, delivering them to their rooms. It didn't last long. The college authorities got wind of my enterprise and banned it on the grounds that it was illegal to operate a business from a hall of residence. I'm pretty sure that what really concerned them was that I was undercutting prices in their refectory, while comfortably beating them on quality.

COPENHAGEN LIVING

So far, my relationship with coffee was one shared by many millions of my generation around the world as we developed tastes and preferences for a drink that had been around for centuries but was now being presented in new ways. I could easily have settled into a routine of drinking decent coffee at home, having a favourite café near my place of work and dropping in on any that looked good while I was out and about. Instead, a couple more twists in my path through life intervened.

The crucial turning point was my decision to study for six months in Copenhagen on a student exchange programme. Denmark may seem an unlikely choice for somebody studying English literature – Shakespeare's great Dane, Prince Hamlet, being perhaps the only strong link – but the courses looked interesting, and Copenhagen had recently emerged as one of the most fashionable cities in the world. René Redzepi's Noma, famous for its foraged ingredients, had been crowned the world's best restaurant three years running (not that I could aspire to eat there on my student budget).

But even if I couldn't eat at Noma, I lived in a beautiful circular hall of residence, Tietgen, designed by Danish architects Lundgaard & Tranberg, based on traditional southern Chinese Hakka buildings and frequently featured in international design magazines. I explored the city on two wheels, joining the throng in the generous bicycle lanes running along every street. It seemed astounding to me that in Denmark, real imagination and investment were put into accommodation for students and cycling infrastructure – both no more than an afterthought back in England. In my Manchester hall of residence, the fittings were ugly, cheap and flimsy, and were treated as such by the students, while I had recently come off second best in a clash with a car on a busy Manchester street. The contrast was absolute: in Tietgen everything was both functional and beautiful, which meant a lot of polished poured concrete, and we students responded in kind with cleaning rotas to ensure our surroundings stayed beautiful. Out on my bicycle, the whole of Copenhagen and its surroundings as far as Hamlet's Elsinore was my oyster.

Wanting to find out more about this city I was falling in love with, I took an optional course in urban design. Around this time, British metropolitan councils were busy setting up bicycle hire schemes and providing cycle lanes in an effort to ease city centre traffic as well as boost health and fitness. Delegations were sent to Copenhagen and other bike-friendly cities like Amsterdam to pick up ideas. I began to dream of working for Gehl Architects, the design practice that had developed Copenhagen's bicycle policy; to dream of becoming an urbanist, transforming cities in Britain and beyond along cycle-friendly Scandinavian lines. I would need qualifications, which I would study for on site – here in Copenhagen. Which is how I came to spend another four years as a student in the city.

Britain was still in the EU at the time and Denmark is generous in its funding of further education, so I did not have to worry about fees for my Masters courses. But I still had to cover my rent and living costs, so part-time work was essential. The solution was pretty straightforward: there were always jobs going in cafés, bars or restaurants.

With its need for evening and weekend staff, hospitality is always a reliably flexible option for students, and pretty soon I was able to pick and choose where I worked. My first stop was an all-day café on the corner of a prosperous neighbourhood near the tourist magnet of Nyhavn. We served drinks and snacks, salads and light lunches, and on quiet days I often worked alone, doing everything from making coffee to rustling up toasted sandwiches and – slowly at first, but with increasing efficiency – clearing the tables. I discovered that by working regularly in one place, you quickly become a familiar face to a large group of regulars; five or more years later, I still bump into people I met at this first café, and we greet each other like old friends.

My next stop was Henrik's Kaffebar in Elmegade, formerly Copenhagen's main fashion drag and still retaining traces of that status, a little like London's Carnaby Street. Over time I graduated to become manager, running the place when Henrik was away and constantly thinking of ways in which it could be improved. Henrik was not a fully paid-up follower of coffee's Third Wave – he held no truck with innovations like non-dairy milk, which are now non-negotiable in a café – but by chance his supplier of Italian coffee beans had let him down so he had switched to a local outfit called Coffee Collective. Meeting them was my inspirational introduction to the science behind coffee making.

Coffee Collective consisted of three guys who had set up shop in Nørrebro, Copenhagen, in 2008, roasting beans sourced directly from growers. They had recently won the world barista championship and were part of a small Scandinavian group, alongside Norway's Tim Wendelboe, in the avant-garde of the global coffee scene. Bizarrely, while being famous in international coffee circles, at home they were still struggling to establish themselves as a viable commercial concern, which meant they were obliged to put a lot of effort into coffee evangelism – into promoting the idea that coffee, like wine, can be an artisan product with an almost infinite palette of tastes, so that each cup can provide a unique experience.

The difference with coffee is that the artisan input occurs not just on the farm – the vineyard and its production facility, the winery – but in two further stages: at the roastery and in the coffee shop. Coffee Collective went to great pains to demonstrate what they were doing as roasters, and to educate baristas in the skills and knowledge required to tease out the best flavours from the beans.

I took full advantage of the opportunities, accompanying staff to two or three of Coffee Collective's barista workshops, which rapidly expanded my knowledge – and my ambitions. I also got to know Callum, an Australian responsible at the time for the company's wholesale operations, who opened my eyes to many aspects of the industry. Without really knowing it, I was beginning to put together my own coffee network, my entry into a community that now – thanks to the advantages of social media – straddles the globe.

THE LIMITED APPEAL OF A PROPER CAREER

I was still working part-time for Henrik by the time I completed my Master's degree and took the first tentative steps on my intended career in urban planning. I managed to nab a short-term perch at Copenhagenize, a multi-disciplinary consultancy in urban bicycle culture, doing the classic menial tasks doled out to interns in offices the world over. My colleagues were interesting and sympathetic, but within a matter of weeks it dawned on me that being holed up with the same group of people every day was frankly dull compared with the buzz of a café. I realised I missed the bustle of service, the satisfaction of feeling in control of a busy coffee shop through the ebb and flow of a day's work, the exchanges with multiple customers and – yes – the compliments and the appreciation of a job done well.

Work was in a shared office space equipped with proper coffee-making equipment, but since it was communal and nobody felt responsible, it was never cleaned or serviced. Aficionado that I had become, I took to bringing in my own AeroPress and ground beans in order to knock up a tasty cup. Colleagues enquired why I bothered, and I soon found myself giving a coffee workshop to the entire workforce – another sign, perhaps, of where my true direction lay.

I persisted for a while in my pursuit of a proper 'career', and managed to book job interviews with a couple of consultancies in London. But whatever their stated principles and motivation, the truth is that money talks, so these niche urban planning consultancies do much of their bread-and-butter work for massive developments and civil engineering projects such as the HS2 high-speed railway. So much for cycle-friendly cities. My dream job at Gehl Architects seemed as far beyond my reach as ever.

If I was serious about switching my career aspirations to coffee, I realised I would have to up my game – which brought me to Forloren, a tiny café run by Nils, a coffee fanatic from an older generation who had spent a few years living in Japan and was inspired by the tiny, ultra-specialist restaurants he had visited there where the proprietor, typically working alone, would serve just one dish – but that dish brought to the highest levels of perfection and consistency. Forloren was not really a commercial vehicle for Nils – more a passion project that he would indulge in for a few years before taking his retirement. Street photography was another of his passions, so the walls of his minimalist café were hung with prime examples from his personal collection.

The coffee itself was put on a pedestal: Nils selected beans from a variety of specialist roasters and his attention to detail in the brewing was second to none. He loved to engage with customers, responding to questions about provenance or roasting or brewing methods in great detail, even if there was a queue waiting to be served. This was deliberately, self-consciously slow coffee – the very opposite of the fast-service ethos of most takeaways.

So I was flattered when Nils agreed to take me on and train me in his methods. He even had a refractometer to measure the levels of extraction in each cup, and I wasn't allowed to make filter coffees for customers until I could consistently match his levels – which made it all the more reward-ing when he gave me the go-ahead to man the machines, and even let me run the café in his absence.

I was happy at Forloren, honing my skills and deepening my knowl-edge and appreciation of coffee every day. Given its purist approach, it was the sort of place that attracts industry insiders, and working there gets you noticed in the right places. Soon enough, I was head-hunted by Oliver, who ran Democratic, one of the best coffee shop/bakeries in Copenhagen, famous for its croissants. He enticed me with tales of the guys who had worked for him: Joe Fisher, an English barista who was now competing in competitions around the world; Jonas Gehl, who had set up Prolog.

By this point I had become seriously ambitious. I knew that a career in coffee would never bring me the material rewards enjoyed by school friends now in finance or the law – but I wasn't motivated by money so much as wanting to make my mark in a field that stimulated me. Coffee had become my calling, much in the way it was for the trio behind Coffee Collective.

While Forloren was tiny, bespoke, low-key, Democratic was quite the opposite: a big, high-volume place with constant queues that required a high level of efficiency and an economy of movement and teamwork from staff in order to maintain a 'good flow' – that optimal level of service in which you knock out consistently delicious cups of coffee for several hours through a shift. It is hard and repetitive work, requiring a high level of fully engaged attention from the barista.

Nobu, the head of coffee or manager at Democratic, had moved to Denmark from Japan a few years earlier, speaking little English and less Danish, to immerse himself in the world of Scandinavian coffee. He liked to dispense nuggets of coffee-shop wisdom – 'the customer is a mirror to the self: if somebody is rude to you, it's because you were rude to them' – and was a truly inspirational figure, showing by his example the gravity of what coffee could offer. For him, coffee was a life-defining obsession that always offered something more to learn. While I was there, Nobu won the Danish roasting championships, and I could see the aura that exposure created: aficionados came from far and wide to taste his coffees, while a steady stream of industry insiders dropped by to ask his advice on one coffee topic or another.

While the coffee side of the operation was certainly impressive, there were frustrating aspects to working at Democratic. For instance, the ice machine worked well enough in the winter, but in the summer when we really needed ice, the machine just couldn't cope. It was company policy to serve a latte in a heatproof glass cup – fair enough, but we only had three of them, so we would chase around the café to grab each one and wash it as soon as the drink was finished. Inadequacies of this type matter: they translate into fewer iced coffees sold, fewer lattes. I was learning what to do when I started my own place – and what not to do.

A DREAM BECOMES A POP-UP REALITY

By now I had mastered the art and intricacies of making consistently good coffee, and had learnt to cope with volume in frantically busy places. But I was becoming increasingly frustrated by the limitations of working for somebody else, to their agenda. There are only so many suggestions you can make, it seemed to me, before you begin to feel you're making a nuisance of yourself. Increasingly, I day-dreamed about opening something of my own – perhaps a mobile coffee cart that I could operate as a side project on my evenings or weekends off, or during the many summer festivals in and around Copenhagen.

One day, a chef I hardly knew began chatting to me over his morning coffee. He was lined up to cater for an event and needed somebody to look after the coffee: would I be interested? I said yes without even thinking about it. How could I refuse, given my vague but insistent plans? He was not fazed when I admitted that I had no equipment at all. So I had a couple of weeks to lay my hands on a cheap grinder, to lease a small coffee machine and throw together the few other odds and ends I would need. Scarlett, my partner, helped me out on the day and luckily for us it rained, so instead of the 100 guests we had planned for, only 50 turned up.

We survived, and my own tiny coffee business was now up and running. I set up at several pop-up street markets and car boot sales, at an events space hosting a clothing sale, and on each occasion I bought the best beans I could lay my hands on from independent roasters so I could serve top-of-the-range coffee from my funky little stall. The approach seemed to work: customers began to notice the quality and complimented me, asking where I was setting up next. I tagged the roasteries I was using in my Instagram feeds, and they tagged me back to their followers – mutual back-scratching that benefits both sides. I was already beginning to build a profile as a participant in the industry, however small – somebody who really cared about coffee.

The need to find a permanent base was now developing a measure of urgency. But what could I possibly afford in a notoriously expensive city? How could I afford to pay commercial rent and rates – let alone put down the deposit and provide the business credentials that most landlords require?

4 OPENING THE FIRST DARCY'S KAFFE

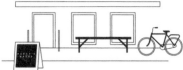

Seven days to launch; what's in a name?; regular customers; the minimum set-up; true independence; staking your pitch.

I knew from the very beginning that my fledgling business was going to be a shoestring operation. I had no money at all, and had never managed to save any. Nor could I expect any funding from my parents, who had chipped in for the occasional plane ticket over the years and didn't have deep enough pockets for anything more. And I certainly had neither the contacts nor the proven track record to take out a bank loan or attract private investment, even if I had wanted them.

For a while, I assumed that it would be simply impossible to find a location where I could afford the rent – let alone the premium that I would have to pay in advance to secure it. So the most I could aspire to in the short-to-medium term was a mobile service catering to special events and even, perhaps, Copenhagen's first fully mobile coffee cart.

Here I should explain for the first, but probably not the last, time how important it is to be open and enthusiastic rather than secretive and private about your plans to open a coffee shop – which is, after all, a community service and not a get-rich-quick scam. Friends and strangers – including people already in the coffee trade – actively *want* you to succeed and will be surprisingly happy to help you out with advice and tips, sometimes even more.

The first of many breaks came when I mentioned my frustration at being unable to secure a permanent site to an architect friend, Anita. Her practice was moving out of its ground-floor office, she told me, and there was a possibility I could take it over without paying a deposit.

As can be imagined, I jumped at the opportunity. The premises were not ideal by any means: the location was tucked away down a side street with little passing traffic by foot, bicycle or car, at lower ground-floor/basement level, rather cold, dark and stark, with a grey tiled floor. But it was affordable, available, I could move in straight away if I wanted to – and frankly, beggars can't be choosers. There were upsides, too: a side room at the back meant that my partner, Scarlett – an architect with her own practice – could have an office, which saved us some money, and it was in a reasonably accessible part of the city, so plenty of potential customers were nearby.

At this point, we went into overdrive. Scarlett scoured Gumtree and Facebook Marketplace for furniture, and cobbled together a bar from four Ikea cupboards that we could put the coffee machine on. There was a rudimentary kitchen out the back but no proper plumbing or sink at the bar, so I set up what was essentially my mobile system with two large 18-litre bottles, one for the water used to make coffee and tea, the other to take waste. I got hold of enough milk jugs to enable me to make a succession of hot drinks without having to dash out the back to wash up, and we were even given an unwanted sofa so customers could relax.

Given that I already had a leased coffee machine, a supply of coffee and a cheap grinder from my mobile set-up, I was able to step up to a bricks-and-mortar site for an immediate outlay of no more than £150. Somehow or other, within seven days of receiving the keys I was open for business.

WHAT'S IN A NAME?

Naming your coffee shop is very important: it is part of your brand identity and ideally is simple, memorable, and identifies the business as a coffee shop.

The most famous coffee shop brand is obviously Starbucks, which takes its name, rather bizarrely, from a character in the American classic novel *Moby Dick*. It is certainly better than Ishmaels or Ahabs, two other potential names from the same source, and I suppose both 'star' and 'bucks' (as slang for dollars) are useful associations.

I agonised for a long time over what I was going to call my coffee shop when it was still no more than a pipedream. Then I went on holiday to France and was struck by the straightforward simplicity of the names of so many of the small, independent cafés and restaurants: Chez Louis, Bar Renaud, Bistro Philippe and so on.

Using a personal name is a useful signifier that the business is independent and owner-operated – with the suggestion that you will be hosted on a personal basis once inside. I grew up near a famous restaurant in south London, Chez Bruce, which used the same device to good effect. And I happen to have a relatively unusual first name (thanks, Mum and Dad!), which these days is fashionably non-gendered.

Kaffe is an interesting and universally understood word in itself, the Danish version of a word that crops up in different languages – as coffee, café, caffè, kaffee, kahve and so on – with two separate but obviously related meanings: the drink coffee, and the premises where it is consumed. In Danish, the word refers only to the drink, so Darcy's Kaffe translates as 'Darcy's Coffee', not 'Darcy's Café'. It is also the case that there is no apostrophe in the written Danish possessive – so the name would be correctly spelt 'Darcys Kaffe' in Danish.

All these confusions are fine – they are part of the calculation – given that the name is so simple and the nature of the business is abundantly clear whatever language you speak. That was my thinking, anyway, and now I'm stuck with it...

Very soon, I had a visit from the council's food and hygiene inspectors. They were perfectly reasonable and didn't make any outrageous demands – but rules are rules, and they did stipulate that I needed to install a second door so there were two doors between the toilet and the coffee shop.

I was so cash-strapped at this stage that I could only afford to have the work done bit by bit as I saved up for components, which led to an excruciating incident which luckily I can laugh at now. A second cousin from Melbourne had dropped in one morning and was the only customer, so I asked her if she would mind the till while I popped out the back to answer a call of nature. Unthinkingly, I shut the two doors behind me – forgetting that the second door did not yet have a handle on the inside. So I was trapped in the toilet, with no way of getting a message to my cousin. Finally, after much fruitless banging on the door and shouting, I managed to squeeze out of a high window and drop into the yard at the back, before making my way round and back into the café by the front door. Such are the perils of a one-man show!

Once the door handles had been fitted, my first major expense was to relocate the bar to the back of the room so it was closer to the sink in the small kitchen. In the kitchen, we swapped out the single-basin sink for a double model that would allow us to allocate one for washing hands and one for cleaning dishes. If we planned to add food preparation at a future stage, we would need to add a third sink for the washing of salad leaves and so on.

OUR FIRST REGULARS

As I became familiar with the quirks of what I had been warned was a slightly dodgy area, the sometimes amusing antics of local characters became familiar. Trickiest was a guy living upstairs who would occasionally wander into the café looking for a light for the spliff he was brandishing; I let him know as politely as I could that we were a no-smoking zone – not my rules, but municipal policy for any café in Copenhagen. Sometimes I would catch sight of him throwing petrol over a fire in the yard; I just hoped no customers happened to be looking.

The trickle of customers finding their way to Darcy's Kaffe – friends, contacts from the other places I had worked in, the occasional passer-by – slowly turned into what I can only describe as a slightly larger trickle. Those who came in seemed to like the improvised space we had created. They would hang around and chat over their coffee, and they came back – my very first regulars. Coffee shops are brilliant in terms of feedback: to a much greater extent than pubs, bars or restaurants, where people tend to come in pairs or packs, bringing their own atmosphere; coffee drinkers often turn up on their own, and are more than willing to exchange pleasantries and let you know what they enjoyed about their visit.

I also discovered the immense power of social media as a marketing tool, almost by accident. Like most people of my generation, I get much of the information I need about daily life from the internet and Instagram feeds, but this had always seemed a large and amorphous territory to me: on the one hand, the 20 to 30 friends I am in regular contact with and the four or five websites I use for information on where to eat in a strange town; on the other hand, the vast global network of millions of people attached to their pocket computers.

So here was I, a tiny new coffee shop in an obscure side street, but I was buying coffee supplies from some of the best and most respected roasteries, and that made me instantly interesting to a whole cohort of coffee enthusiasts. One of the roasteries was Koppi in Helsingborg, a small Swedish city not far from Copenhagen, directly across the Øresund Strait from Helsingør (Hamlet's Elsinore). Koppi opened in 2007 as a coffee shop and began roasting its own beans a few years later, becoming one of the biggest noises on the Scandinavian coffee scene. Co-founder Anne Lunell kindly agreed to sit down with me over a meal and give me a few tips on how to run a coffee shop.

She also gave a shout-out to Darcy's Kaffe on the Koppi Instagram feed, which is read by 70,000 followers. The effect was quite dramatic, given that it took only a tiny percentage of those followers who happened to be in Copenhagen – and bothered to take up the recommendation – to produce a visible spike in the number of new faces coming through my door over the next few days.

One of those faces belonged to André Kaliff, a dancer-turned-forager and one half of a foodie couple (his wife Camilla Skov has written two bestselling Danish cookbooks) who has become one of my best friends and closest collaborators at Darcy's Kaffe. Within weeks André was doing pop-ups with us, producing an amazing and original take on a Swedish waffle that he could rustle up on our tiny domestic machine. We would put word out that he was doing something on a Saturday, and it would invariably sell out within a couple of hours. This was good business in itself, of course, but also helped establish a bit of an aura around Darcy's Kaffe as a basement that had good things going on – the sort of hidden gem people like to know about.

Another customer who walked in off the street one day became a friend and then, soon enough, the first person I employed. Dan offered to look after the shop every now and then so I could take a day off – a good move for my sanity, for my relationship, and also vital in terms of networking: I could meet suppliers, visit roasteries and attend to all the 101 little things that I couldn't attend to while serving cups of coffee. And this, of course, would all feed back into social media shout-outs from people in the coffee trade.

So far, then, the early days of Darcy's Kaffe might read like a smooth and untroubled ascent, a business that grew organically on its own terms from day one, generating its own momentum while I sat back and enjoyed the ride. That might even be a reasonably accurate description of it in the long, sweeping view: a graph that headed slowly but steadily in the right direction. But much of the time it felt anything but, and on many mornings I really had to force myself to get out of bed in the dark and head out in the cold Copenhagen pre-dawn to open up in time for the first breakfasts to be served at 8 a.m. For the first six months or so I was working every day as a one-man band, spending all day on my feet then racing around on a heavy cargo bike for an hour or more after closing to pick up supplies of water, milk, coffee and more. I was physically shattered and lost 10 kilos.

THE MINIMUM SET-UP

You can – people do – spend thousands of pounds on some very fancy coffee-making kit to equip your new coffee shop. But you don't need to. Here is a list of what I believe are the absolute minimum requirements, which need cost no more than a couple of hundred pounds/euros/dollars.

- **Espresso machine.** You need something to make coffee with. Obviously. You could go down the route of Born Drippy, a Japanese-style joint in London that only served hand-brewed filter coffee, so all they needed was a grinder and a kettle. But this was highly specialised and struggled against the demand for espresso-based drinks. Espresso machines can be expensive. You don't *need* to buy top of the range and you don't *need* to buy new, but just be careful of the condition. There are plenty of speciality coffee marketplaces, such as United Baristas. After trying a number of different brands (Nuova Simonelli, Astoria, Synesso) I favour the simplicity and reliability of La Marzocco. I started with the smallest (commercial standard) machine possible, the Linea Mini, and grew to a two-group Linea Standard and a three-group PB – both purchased second-hand.
- **Grinder(s).** This is where people (I include myself in this group) skimp, but that is a mistake. There is a lot of truth in the saying, 'You're only as good as your grinder.' But sometimes you feel you have no choice. I had spent all my money on the lease agreement for the Linea Mini (there is often a significant start-up fee for these lease agreements) and all I could afford for a grinder was a 'cheap' Anfim prosumer model (still around €350 [£304]). It felt sturdy enough and looked the part, gleaming with stainless steel. However, when

it came to the important matter of grinding, it suffered. The first shot would be OK, but then as soon as it came to the second and the third, the shots would become increasingly erratic and speedy as the burrs started to heat up. This is why commercial grinders are so big: the burrs are a bit bigger, but the motor and cooling tech are what really add to the bulk. Once I could afford a second-hand Mythos grinder from Nuova Simonelli, everything became more consistent. And don't let it come as a shock that you will need a separate grinder for filter brewing. These can vary wildly in price but you get what you pay for. I would recommend something like a Wilfa Uniform (circa €200 [£174]) to start with while you save up for the industry-standard Mahlkönig EK43 (circa €2,000 [£1,738] new or slightly cheaper second-hand).

- **Water system.** This can range from the humble festival set-up all the way up to a state-of-the-art reverse osmosis (RO) system. It all depends on your local water supply, your ambition with coffee (everyday neighbourhood level or standout) and of course budget. Most water companies (BWT and Pentair being two of the global leaders) will offer rental agreements on their systems.
- **Milk pitchers.** These don't need to be fancy latte art brands, but a range of sizes would be good (see Chapter 6 for more on this).
- **Scales.** Again, there's no need to go for the higher-end brands or models. But ideally, something built for coffee bars that is responsive, accurate to 0.1 g and waterproof (or at least claims to be). It will be helpful, if not essential, to have a small one for using with the espresso machine and a larger one to weigh the portafilter (+ coffee).
- **Cups.** Both to stay and take away, depending on your business (although I personally think every place serving coffee should try to have some non-disposable cups for those lingering es-presso quaffers). I have always used one of the industry leaders in specialised coffee cups, Acme of New Zealand, but there are several companies producing cups to suit a range of budgets and styles. The old-school latte/piccolo glasses from French

brand Duralex are also a good option on a budget. Takeaway cups should be checked for sustainability, quality of cup and lid (do they spill, break down etc) and whether they can be stamped or printed (see Chapter 11 on the marketing value of branded cups).

- **Fridge.** For milk and cold drinks. I started out with a cheap domestic one that did the job. But note that the constant opening and closing of the fridge door is not good for these types of fridges (or any really for that matter). We now use commercial fridges that fit neatly under the bar top and can store many more litres (we get deliveries of 45 litres of milk at least twice a week). Note that non-dairy milk alternatives don't need to be chilled until they are opened. This should save you space. Freezer space would be great for keeping ice cold for iced lattes, but you can get a cool box in the meantime and buy ice in bags as a starting point.

- **POS system – aka point-of-sale system.** You need something that will enable you to take payments efficiently and effectively. There are a number of companies offering a fresh way to do this for very little up-front expense (think Zettle, SumUp, Square, among many others). Look for one that takes the lowest per-centage of your sales (and try to negotiate that figure down as your sales increase) and offers a good deal on their card machines. Hopefully it looks good, works quickly and can last all day unplugged.

- **Cleaning tools.** Both for the coffee machine and for everything else. Ensuring you have a well-organised and stocked cleaning supply will help to ensure that cleanliness is maintained and machines last longer. Make sure you research and show the team how to clean the machines properly so you don't end up losing screws and having an unwelcome surprise when you open the café one morning (this has happened too many times to mention for us).

- And finally, the **coffee.** This is obviously one of the key pieces of the puzzle to try and get right when you open but there are many different approaches you can take so it deserves its own section...

Pros and cons of a deal with a supplier

When you start out your coffee biz maybe you already have in mind some coffee roasters that you want to work with. Maybe you've had beans from them at home and enjoyed how they tasted. Perhaps you've been following them on Instagram and like what they represent and how they approach their business. Whatever it is that draws you to a particular roaster, it's good to make contact with them as early as possible and begin a dialogue about becoming a customer of theirs. You need to see if setting up an account is possible (small-scale or micro roasters have a limit on how many cafés they can provide coffee to) and then the essentials: the prices they can give on coffee for wholesale accounts, what the arrangements are (roasting and delivery days, order cut-offs, payment terms etc). Depending on the scale of the roastery you connect with, they might be able to help you out with more than just quality coffee.

The bigger, more established roasteries might be able to help with equipment advice and training, custom roasts, and even stretch to loaning machinery and/or helping to set up leasing agreements through their network of distributors. Whatever they might offer on this side of things will usually come with some sort of agreement on collaboration, making your relationship less that of a friend helping a friend and more of a business transaction. Especially if equipment is part of the equation, the roastery will want to get their investment back and lock you into a (probably written) binding agreement that will ensure a certain level of exclusivity and potentially even minimum order requirements.

The upside of this kind of deal is that you can get up and running very quickly and thoroughly with a good level of machinery, without the capital investment that would otherwise be necessary. Connecting your fledgling business with an established player in the coffee scene might also be beneficial in giving your site credibility and exposure if they post on their channels about you.

The drawback to locking yourself into business with one provider is that you lose your ability to be flexible and dynamic with your offering. In some way, you compromise your independence as, even though your café is your own baby, it risks appearing as an offshoot of the roastery. In some big markets such as London, there are numerous new, independent coffee shops that end up losing their individual identity somewhat as they have the same coffee in their grinders as their neighbours. This might not matter to every shop – it depends what your focus is on. If your emphasis is on your food or baked goods, or magazines for that matter, the uniqueness of the coffee you serve may be less significant, so long as it is tasty and your customers enjoy it.

SETTING OUT YOUR STALL

Decide what type of coffee shop you want to create, and how to go about achieving that target.

For my own part, I was super into coffee; more than that, I was super into the *world* around coffee – the stories, the brands, the personalities and so on. So I wanted to make my humble contribution to that story – to create a space where people would feel comfortable and relaxed, but also have access to new and exciting coffee experiences, so they could discover for themselves just how crazily diverse coffee could be. If they were already converts, signed-up members of the coffee tribe, then they could come to a like-minded place and potentially discover something new.

This meant I couldn't lock myself into an agreement with a particular roaster, no matter how potentially lucrative that would be for me. It went against the core concept. I would change supplier on a regular basis (pretty much roaster of the week) and I gradually built up a rotating line-up of roasting 'partners' who I trusted to give me and my customers something first of all consistent (in their roasting and quality control), but also something different that would showcase the range of coffee experiences (origins, processes, approaches to roasting – omni, light-medium, or pretty much everything except for dark). This diversity in our curating was soon reflected in the growth of our retail sales. We became known as *the* place for buying interesting coffees that were nigh on impossible to find elsewhere, meaning that coffee geeks would check in on a regular basis, as well as more standard customers buying coffee as a present for the coffee lover in their life. We would always ensure we had a range on offer to suit every taste and budget – not just high-grown Ethiopian heirloom varieties or award-winning Panamanian geishas but also solid Brazilian or Costa Rican beans that would suit the bung-it-in-a-cafétiere customer. Every now and again we would offer the latter customer a sample of something a little more racy and elegant, to see if we could tempt them – always keeping it fun and pressure-free.

As my café was born out of this burning passion for all things coffee, I didn't really consider any other format for the shop to take. However, if you're not as motivated by pure coffee enthusiasm as I am, don't despair. There's plenty of business (and fun) to be had from being friendly and welcoming, and serving up the best cup of coffee you can. Most coffee shops around the world earn their crust from flat whites, iced lattes and Americanos (mine included), so the best thing to do is focus on serving these as well as you can (see Chapters 6 and 9) and build up a base of returning customers with your levels of hospitality. A smile, a joke and an acknowledgement can go a long way to winning over a new customer, whatever style or format your business takes. Make an effort with people, even if your business is centred around the lightning-fast transactions of a takeaway kiosk.

5 BUILDING A PROPER BUSINESS

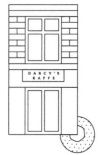

Partnership woes; the Carlsberg pop-up; building a team; farewell to the basement; a new home; surviving Covid; a second branch; baking.

As the months passed, Scarlett and I carried on trying to improve the basement, both aesthetically and practically. When there was a little money left over after paying the rent and invoices, we would source out better-quality second-hand furniture and I managed to secure a payment arrangement with the lovely people at Coffee Collective for a new grinder (the omnipresent EK43 by Mahlkönig) that would allow me to brew filter coffee to a much higher standard, as well as grind retail bags for customers much more effectively.

For a period, we hosted an avant-garde magazine shop specialising in fashion, art and hard-to-find publications, in an attempt to save some money on the rent and to attract more customers. This proved ill-fated as the owner of the other fledgling business turned out to be a nightmare – not paying his share of rent or his suppliers (among them local artists and makers), resulting in frequent visits from stressed, out-of-pocket creditors inquiring about the whereabouts of my 'partner'.

This situation dragged on for about six months, eventually resolving itself when he moved on to what would prove to be another ill-fated space, but it taught me some valuable lessons. I still believe collaborations are potentially a great way to kick-start a new business – sharing resources and costs, boosting each other's reputations and footfall – and that coffee and magazines are a classic combination. Where I went wrong was that I did not know enough about who I was going into business with. I had no idea how unpredictable he would prove to be, how selfish and damaging his behaviour. At its worst, this was the only period in the café's existence to date when I honestly felt like not going into work each day – when I seriously felt that packing it in might be the best step. It put pressure not only on me and my professional life, but also on my relationship with Scarlett (the two of them fell out big time).

If my first mistake was not doing my homework on this person, the second and potentially more significant error was not getting a contract drawn up between us and our companies. Regardless of how well you know somebody, it is always a good idea to have something down on paper and signed, if only to avoid any miscommunication or misunderstandings. At worst, the contract might be necessary as the basis for any legal proceedings that need to be threatened or carried out.

A POP-UP IN A (FORMER) BREWERY

In a happier period of the basement era of Darcy's Kaffe, we set up a pop-up coffee shop in a newly created neighbourhood of Copenhagen at the old Carlsberg brewery, snuggled up next to Frederiksberg and Vesterbro. As happens in large-scale new development areas in cities around the world, a consultancy was commissioned to create a vibrant slice of city life here, and the task of curating a healthy mix of retail spaces was a big part of their plans. I was contacted by this consultancy, who ran through the prospectus with me and subsequently introduced me to the Carlsberg bosses, who had to sign off on prospective tenants. What I came to realise through this process was that, just as much as I needed to impress them with talk of my aesthetics and the quality of coffee and service that I would be offering to their new residential tenants, they were trying to impress me with the opportunity they were offering.

For you have to realise that opening up a shop, even just a temporary space, is a massive investment – mostly in time. They really wanted to attract an independent operator who would offer a different quality and atmosphere than they could achieve with a branch of an established chain – something that would give new residents the feeling that they were living in a real, authentic city district, not something faceless and soulless. In the end, they offered me the space rent-free, and they even helped pay some of the start-up costs so we could do a simple fit-out without dipping into my limited funds. Before this experience, I would never have imagined this would be possible; if a similar opportunity comes along now, I will be confident in my requests.

We had a really good summer in this pop-up space with some busy days knocking out mainly takeaway coffee along with ice cream in pots from a local company that lent me a retail freezer. As I now had two sites to cover, it forced me to expand the team even though I was still working as many days as I had before. We had a couple of part-timers who could put in more hours as needed in the summer, when it was busier and they were on vacation from university. One of these new recruits, Jacob Lund, proved to be indispensable and came back to work for the café two years later, while also becoming a key part of the Noma front-of-house team.

When the days began to get shorter and darker – which happens with dramatic force in Copenhagen, as far north as Edinburgh and Moscow – the pop-up shop experienced quieter days, and the lack of a cosy seating area really began to drag business down. When the time came to discuss a possible extension, I decided not to go for it.

Around this time I also came across a promising site just around the corner from the basement in Nørrebro, where by now I had built up a steady stream of regulars and some decent weekend action, helped by André's now famous 'weekend walk in the woods' waffles. The Carlsberg pop-up had taught me some valuable lessons. I had learnt about the logistical difficulties imposed by having two sites. The amount of times I had to transport heavy or unwieldy items across town on my bike (19 litres of water is no joke!), or enlist the services of Christian, my friend with a similarly nascent cargo bike delivery business called Onward, hammered home this new challenge.

HIRING AND TRAINING

This was also the time I really started to build a proper team, hiring people I felt I could trust to do the job when I wasn't around. Training was something that I hadn't really considered before, but I had taken on some less experienced baristas so I was forced to develop some structure to induct them into the business. These early employees will probably testify to the well-intentioned but messy training sessions that were more of a jolly get-together than a brewing boot camp. To be fair, the importance of these meet-ups should not be dismissed. A team that gets along socially and has some shared memories is much more likely to gel on the shop floor and work effectively together. And customers will definitely pick up on an atmosphere – either good or bad.

With this expanding team across multiple sites, it became clear that communication was key in order for things to run smoothly. Nowadays we use the instant messaging program Slack to communicate effectively across the different departments and locations, but in the early days it was a mix of handwritten notes left for the person opening the café and Facebook Messenger threads that grew increasingly unwieldy.

An early regular customer who became a friend, Peter, who runs a great local pasta joint with two sites (Bar Pasta), once told me that he asks every member of staff to write something down about how the service was that evening, even if it was uneventful, as a means of promoting communication within the team. I know exactly what he is getting at: the key is to establish a good pattern of talking early on, so that it becomes completely normal and part of the culture to pass on relevant information, at all times.

The café world is different from the restaurant world, in which you might have a team meeting every day and share a 'family meal' before evening service, where you can pass on messages and swap stories. So with a coffee shop you need to make an extra effort to ensure all the team is clued in on what is happening. This is even more relevant if you have part-timers on board, as they miss out on everything that takes place on the days when they are not working.

As well as this learning experience, the pop-up shop exposed me to a new audience on the other side of town (only 15 minutes by bicycle but that's a lot by Copenhagen standards). While I wouldn't see many of these new customers back in Nørrebro, it proved to be helpful in time to have built up a little following over in Vesterbro/Frederiksberg.

NEW MARKETS

My taste of a shop with a better location was intoxicating, and now I was on the look-out for a permanent move. I knew in my heart that the basement spot was always going to be a struggle, despite the loyal crew of regulars who surprisingly claimed it as their personal hidden gem.

My feeling was confirmed by my mum's partner MJ, herself an experienced businesswoman, when they visited. They were proud of what I had created but they had the place (and me) to themselves. Nice to catch up, of course, but not a great sign that the business was thriving. MJ would later take me to one side and tell me, as sensitively as she could, that the basement was never going to be a real business. She complimented the food, coffee and service I was providing, and Scarlett's design choices, but said these efforts were wasted in a site so hidden away. Generously, she promised to try to help me pay a deposit for another site, if I could find one that was significantly better. This definitely gave me a kick up the backside, and I'd like to thank MJ for that timely pep talk.

I had bookmarked on my computer all the estate agents that handled business leases, combing through their properties with impatience for the combination of affordability and quality that I was looking for. My requirements were fairly conventional: street level (I was thoroughly done with basement life), natural light, visibility and passing traffic (preferably on foot or bicycle). Size-wise, I wasn't too picky but my budget dictated that I would have to go for a modest layout. As well as trawling the web, I would walk and cycle around different neighbourhoods to get a feel for them, keeping my eye out with an increasing sense of desperation for promising empty sites.

In fact, what I was looking for ended up being just around the corner from me. I had spotted a bike shop that looked like it was closing down, just five minutes' walk from the basement. It was on a corner, a slight step down from street level and with lots of tall windows along almost the entire length of the shop. It was narrow but long, and peeking through the windows I could see wooden floorboards that needed a sand and clean but looked promising. There was an inconspicuous note in the window that simply read 'Shop for rent. 110m² plus a basement', with a contact email address that I could work out was for a cooperative.

Without going into too much detail, a fairly large percentage of the housing in Copenhagen is run cooperatively, whereby residents buy into the cooperative via a modest flat purchase and then pay a small rent every month. They run the building's finances together as a group, with elected board members meeting every so often to decide on steps that the building needs to take – investments, repairs, rules and regulations and so on. A lot of residential buildings in Copenhagen have a commercial space on the ground floor, and in the case of cooperatives – or *andelsbolig* – they are also in control of the activities going on there, deciding what kind of business they want to rent the space. This also means that the rent is generally more reasonable than with a standard commercial landlord, who simply wants to get the highest income.

I thought the site was promising, but wasn't convinced. I was looking at some other possibilities that I thought would have more traffic, including one near a very busy bakery called Juno. I also had a dialogue going with a design shop (Frama) that was looking for a partner to run an in-house café. However, when this stalled I took my good friend Christian Saxeide (of the bike delivery outfit) to look at the shop after a dinner nearby – and he made my mind up for me.

Christian is somebody whose opinion I value. He works with hospitality businesses, transporting and delivering from suppliers to restaurants, coffee shops and bars. He's also a local guy who had been living on Rantzausgade for over a decade and had witnessed it transform from quite an unpleasant and dodgy street – narrow pavements, car traffic whizzing past and a visible gang presence – into a more relaxed thoroughfare with a huge increase in bicycle traffic after some interventions in the public realm by the municipality (Copenhagen is good with that) and the opening of a couple of shops and bars with a focus on quality. The gangs seemed to have moved on. One of the first high-quality cocktail bars in the city was thriving on Rantzausgade (it now houses a restaurant with a Michelin star, JATAK), there was a great beer bar and restaurant – but there was still no coffee shop. That's not entirely true. There was one directly opposite, but it was a chain operation that did not focus on quality or atmosphere, more on student deals and providing a quiet work space. Some people I spoke to about the site queried the decision to open so close to another coffee business, but I wasn't worried. We would be doing two completely different things. At the time this was the quieter end of the street, but as Christian pointed out, there was *a lot* of bicycle traffic coming off the main road just adjacent and heading up through Nørrebro.

Scarlett and I put together a little presentation about the site, partly to crystallise our own thoughts about the potential, partly so I could show MJ that I had indeed located the better site that she had instructed me to find. We mentioned the bike traffic numbers, helpfully recorded every few years by Copenhagen municipality (who put it at 8,000 a day). We mentioned the prominent corner position that seemed to benefit from a healthy exposure to mid-morning sun. We also highlighted the size of the unit, which would allow us to build a bigger food preparation area, have a proper dishwashing space and also seat a lot more people than we could ever have squeezed into the basement.

A presentation was also drawn up to convince the board of the co-operative that we were the best prospective tenants to take over the shop. Luckily they were looking for something that would increase the life around the building – which gave us a distinctive advantage over the office and studio that had so far applied. Also in our favour was the fact that key board members knew our basement shop, were fans of what we were doing down there and wanted us closer to home. This was a lucky circumstance and it's yet another testament to the importance of engaging with all of your customers. You never know who you're serving and when you'll bump into them again.

MOVING HOUSE

Better still, given that this was not a commercial transaction with a conventional landlord, there was no requirement to pay a deposit. As quickly as possible, we sealed the deal.

Once we had reached agreement with our landlords at the basement on ending our tenure there, it was time to move. The cooperative was prepared to sand and oil the wooden floors, which had taken a bit of a beating when the premises was a bike mechanic's workshop (there are still screws to be found between some of the floorboards in the back room), and also give the walls a fresh coat of white paint. This reduced the workload quite significantly but we still had a lot to do to transform an empty W-shaped space into a café.

Money was also tight. I simply couldn't afford to close for more than a week or so, as sales were my only source of cash flow and I didn't have any savings to act as a buffer (another harsh lesson learnt). We managed to close the basement on 8 January 2020 and serve our first coffees in the new space barely six days later, on 14 January. The space was far from finished; indeed, looking back at the photos I'm shocked at the minimalism (to describe it generously). But we were in.

A couple of factors made this espresso renovation possible. Firstly, proximity: the two spots were only five minutes apart on foot, through an open Copenhagen courtyard. We were able to walk most of the furniture across, although we had to rent a van for some of the heavier items – which ironically took rather longer than walking in cycle-friendly Copenhagen.

The second factor in our favour was our network, or shall we just say friends. Scarlett's architecture schoolmates proved more helpful than my ragtag social science/humanities friends, but between us we had a pretty handy crew who helped put up shelves and lights and knocked down the odd wall (here's to you, Nick). Our friend Sandy, whom we met through a combination of mutual acquaintances and the basement café, began his working relationship with Scarlett and Darcy's at this point, creating bench-style seating for the many window recesses using wood repurposed from the bar at the Carlsberg pop-up. As for our new bar, I spent the first week with the Linea Mini coffee machine and a grinder sitting on a butcher's block sourced from our local Ikea. My work surface, where I also prepped some basic food, was an out-of-service counter-fridge.

At this stage, the space had limited electrical power and no access at all to plumbing, which meant no fresh water or drainage at the bar. This was far from ideal, obviously, but I could get by using filtered water delivered in 19-litre bottles, with an empty bottle slowly filling up through the day with waste water from the machine. I had to have the Linea Mini connected to the filtered water as the faster-paced flow meant I didn't have the time to pull out the drip tray to fill up its little water tank. This was a short-term 'quick and dirty' solution to open the shop for business as quickly as possible, but I knew that as soon as I had the cash I would be paying a plumber the good money they charge to bring some pipes through the basement and up into the bar, where I would have a filter installed to supply the coffee machine with clean water.

As things were to turn out, I had an enforced closure coming up that nobody could have predicted. Before we get to the dreaded 'C' word, I will just say a few things about those crazy first few weeks in our new space. We were exhausted after our whirlwind six-day move and installation, but for me the hard work was about to really kick in. We were lucky to be busy from day one, partly due to the improved location, but mainly thanks to our wonderful regulars who eagerly came by from opening time onwards to drink their usual coffees in the new, much more spacious surroundings.

Having this steady stream of custom from the outset gave me much-needed energy, as I was so drained that a quiet start might have put me to sleep. It ensured that passers-by, all those cyclists streaming past the windows, would notice that something new was happening on this slightly forgotten corner. Importantly, it gave the new café the kind of start that filled me with confidence that the move had been a good one – that the risk would pay off.

Those opening weeks were great but they were also tough. In my extremely careful optimism I was still essentially a one-man band, at least during service hours. Dan and André would do the occasional hour or two before their shifts at other cafés, while Scarlett and friends would help with dishes at the weekend. We were still having to wash everything by hand using boiling water – which, required by the civic health authorities, is probably not recommended by dermatologists. The skin on my hands suffered terribly and although I discovered a cream at the pharmacy that acted as an invisible glove, my hands wouldn't properly heal from this period until months later. (I also had an unfortunate food-poisoning episode a few days in after an ill-fated celebratory steak burger at a local takeaway – so much for food hygiene! Closing down the next day was not in the plans but I simply had nobody who could step in for me at this early stage.)

COVID STRIKES

After a whirlwind first few weeks at the new Kaffe, during which an electrician had installed the more powerful circuit we needed to power a two-group espresso machine, news began to filter through of the pandemic that would change the world as we all knew it for a couple of mad years. The Danish authorities decreed that almost everything had to shut down, but takeaway businesses were allowed to continue operating provided they conformed to rules about social distancing and reduced contact.

We closed for a single day to work out the new lay of the land, and quickly decided to place a table just inside an open door with a small display of beans and other coffee accessories, to show that we were open while preventing anybody from coming in. I would man the table to take orders, with another table behind me that would carry a selection of pastries and sandwiches for the day. The coffee machine sat against the wall behind that, still on the Ikea butcher's block, where a succession of temporary baristas pumped out coffees. Luckily, we were busy enough to afford staff for the first time.

We kept up the energy and engagement with customers who came by to pick up a takeaway coffee and perhaps a bite to eat, and we were extremely fortunate that the first lockdown was accompanied by a miraculous spell of good weather – the perfect spring that everyone so desperately needed to get through the gloomy experience. To our growing amazement, business actually started to boom. The queue of customers lining up outside the shop grew daily in a kind of self-fulfilling prophecy: the bigger the queue, the more people noticed this new café, and so the word continued to spread. With offices in the city centre closed for the duration, local residents who would usually be absent all week were now working from home, and would pop out for a stroll and a coffee break – to our benefit.

For coffee operators, takeaway trade is in many ways far more profitable than sit-down: you only have to interact with customers for a minute or two and there are no 'hosting' costs. So being closed inside while still having takeaway cash flow meant we could do more work on the shop's interior, finishing what we had started in our 'espresso-reno'. We hired some professional builders to build a kitchen/food prep area behind a half-height wall, with a new floor on top of the alarmingly uneven wooden floorboards. We took the counter-fridge from the bar to form one work surface in the kitchen, and had another bar top from Ikea resting on top of some kitchen cabinetry from the same source.

For the first time, we were now investing in professional craftsmen, but we still tried our best to limit the budget by doing time-consuming and (relatively) low-skill jobs, such as painting, ourselves (although Scarlett will, perhaps a little too vehemently, attest to my lack of ability here). We also managed to adapt cabinets from Ikea to form the base structure of our new bar. This would finally give us a long surface running along the rear wall, which we then had tiled above and sealed, with ample room for storing all the bits and pieces you need at the bar, from coffee beans to takeaway cups and bags.

As the days grew longer and warmer, the pandemic showed signs of abating and it was clear that the lockdowns would begin to relax. We were now ready to invite customers inside what was in essence almost another new shop. We had new tables, a new layout, a new high bar seating area at the back that Sandy had somehow casually put together using more foraged wood. We had a 'proper' food prep area with built-in storage, we had a (just about) working second-hand dishwasher that I had managed to lump into the back of a van with help from Christian (getting drenched in the process). We had a plumbed-in coffee machine with its own filtered water supply from BWT (see Chapter 6 for more details). We had a sink and a pitcher rinser at the bar, so no need for 15 different jugs and frequent runs to the back to clean them. We had actually hired a couple more people for the team due to the busyness of the takeaway operation (there were plenty of experienced hospitality hands in town who had been laid off by restaurants and would have to wait a good while before the restaurant scene recovered).

NEW HORIZONS

We emerged from the trials and tribulations of the pandemic years in a stronger position than we could have dreamed of, with a fantastic team – in fact, almost too many great people who were hungry for work. The time seemed right to look for a second location, and a smaller site in another part of town made sense to me. After all, I'd run the Carlsberg pop-up at a much earlier stage in the Kaffe's evolution, and we were now in a much healthier and more solid state. I didn't want to just roll out a carbon copy, but I was convinced that the core principles of good, interesting coffee, some simple food and friendly, engaged service could be replicated with success elsewhere.

Following the pandemic it was plain to see that there were opportunities out there. Some of it was sad to witness: empty units, closed-down shops and businesses, and new-build blocks that had unoccupied retail units on the ground floor. I did as I had done before, and kept my eye out when cycling through different parts of town as well as periodically trawling through the various estate agents' websites that I knew had up-to-date commercial premises listings.

Eventually I found something I thought suitable, in Frederiksberg: near enough that I could easily commute between the two sites (a 15-minute cycle ride) but far enough away from the Rantzausgade shop (which we now refer to as the 'mothership') not to cannibalise our own business. At almost half the size (60m² vs 110m²), it was significantly smaller than the mothership, so more manageable and requiring fewer staff. Significantly for me at the time, it was already a coffee shop of sorts, so surely wouldn't need renovation on the scale that a former bike shop had required. There were sinks in what seemed the right places and, by extension, plumbing; there was a two-group coffee machine in operation, so there must be sufficiently powerful electricity; and the outgoing tenant even offered me a small commercial dishwasher and fridge that she no longer needed, at a good price. Aside from the lick of paint and general spruce-up that I was sure Scarlett would suggest, the shop seemed almost ready to go, and I could picture myself slinging coffees out of the takeaway window hatch (I had always dreamed of having one of those) in a matter of weeks.

How wrong could I be? Once we got our electricians and plumbers in to take a look (annoyingly, only after we had signed the contract), they informed me that both the plumbing and the electrics had been a hack job and were not only illegal but potentially dangerous for anyone working there or potentially even drinking a coffee… This was a shock and obviously begged the question: what on earth had the previous tenants been up to? As I looked at the plumbing work and inspected it from below in the basement, even I could see what the professionals meant: pipes going from plastic into metal into plastic again; connections taped up where there had obviously been leaks; no gradient to speak of for the waste pipe to do its thing, which would inevitably result in blockages. As for the electrics, the fuse board was tucked away in a pretty inaccessible spot behind a wall and looked like it was from the *Downton Abbey* era – the thought even crossed my mind that it might have some value as a piece of vintage or antique memorabilia.

Incredulous at the costs and delays we were now facing to get this project up and running, I contacted the landlord directly, having only dealt with the estate agent up to then. I explained the situation and made the case that we were going to be improving the space for her for years to come, that this was work that legally had to be done. While I hadn't been able to negotiate a period of free rent (there had been some competition for the lease and all I thought the space needed was a minor facelift), I finally managed to persuade the landlord to agree to split the cost of the work. This still left me with a hefty bill to pay, but I had heard horror stories from other café operators of landlords who refused to contribute anything towards essential works that made their units fit for use – so I bit my tongue and agreed to the terms.

This was not the end of the saga; it sometimes seemed that everything that could go wrong, did go wrong. For instance, the flooring guy went bankrupt halfway through the job, leaving us in the lurch. Finally, after countless delays and setbacks, we were ready to open: what was supposed to have been the 'easiest' of my four launches had taken all of three months – a lot longer than I had wanted and expected, but in the bigger picture, not too bad (many hospitality projects take months and even years to get off the ground).

On the credit side, the shop looked absolutely amazing. Scarlett had completely transformed the space from an anonymous, drab café into the most stylish and considered coffee shop I have ever seen, through her choices of paint and lighting and a collaboration with our friend Sandy at Stance Studio, who designed, built and installed a long central table, a high table in the window and a retail display that wrapped around a large display fridge.

Not everything was in place on the day we opened, but the space was clean and functional from day one. We added long shelves over the bar one evening a few weeks in, which added more layers to the design as well as much-needed storage for the baristas. The small kitchen was the one area we didn't have time or money to fix up during the renovation, so a few weeks in we closed for a couple of days to lay down some better flooring and install an improved work surface and storage. It's still very tight in the small food prep area, with only enough room for one person to work at a time, but it's sufficient to prep and then bang out our simple menu of toasties, granolas with yoghurt, grilled croissants and fresh sandwiches.

We knew we had to make some noise about this second opening. The new Kaffe was in a potentially quite dead location, and while there is the occasional decent restaurant nearby, there had never been a coffee shop of any quality. The nearest good bakery was Hart Bageri more than 15 minutes' walk away and the nearest specialty coffee shop was Prolog in the meatpacking district around 25 minutes away – intimidating distances by the standards of Copenhagen. By now the Darcy's Kaffe Instagram account had around 11,000 followers, which obviously made a good starting point for getting some attention. In the final phase of the rebuild I posted stories from the new site that I hoped would pique interest and create awareness before we opened the doors. We didn't put anything in the window to announce the new business (this is a great idea, I think – next time!) but we made a point of talking to interested passers-by and neighbours when we were on site. We also had a busy shop not far away (35 minutes on foot), full of regulars we would make sure we told about the new branch if they didn't already know.

This was a very ground-level approach but I also had some flyers printed (compostable and plantable – they wouldn't just become litter) that would introduce the new coffee shop in the area and entitled the recipient to a free coffee on the house on their first visit. I gave these out to customers at the mothership and also at events I attended around town.

Hosting events was another good way of spreading awareness of the new Darcy's Kaffe, whose smaller scale and quick close-down time at the end of the normal day's trading made it ideal for an evening tasting or masterclass. The Copenhagen Food Festival takes place early every summer with events across the city, and the organisers invited me to put on something coffee related. Our contribution was a cupping (or tasting) evening and a 'barista basics' event at the new shop, which went so well that we have incorporated a diary of bi-monthly cupping evenings open to the public into our plans.

OUR OWN BAKERY

As we settled in at the new shop and business slowly began to pick up with new regulars – and some old ones reconnecting from the Carlsberg days – we also got to know the shopkeepers who were close neighbours. It always pays to be friendly with those around you for many reasons, but one is that you get to learn of new opportunities first. A neighbour who was running a small business-to-business bakery two doors down quickly became one of our daily regulars, and he mentioned that he was leaving his space to move to a bigger site: were we interested?

Up until this point, we had been increasingly relying on other bakeries to supply us with everything from sourdough buns and loaves of bread to croissants and other laminated pastries. While we baked the cardamom buns, banana bread and Anzac biscuits that were among our bestselling items, we simply didn't have the capacity to do more and meet the increasing demand. Having a production space where we could dedicate staff hours to making doughs and baking would change everything.

So, six months into having the new café, we took over the space two doors down, acquiring the closest thing to a plug-in-and-play bakery. We still needed to do a deep clean of the premises, performing an exorcism of sorts to banish the smell of vanilla (the bakery was a cheesecake specialist: tonnes of Oreo and red velvet had passed through its ovens), and to install some of our own equipment such as new fridges and freezers, a 'proper' mixer and a baking table.

We also had to find somebody to head up this new venture – someone who ideally had experience of running a good-quality bakery. In a city full of bakeries it can actually be difficult to find good bakers to join a team, such is the competition for quality staff. Fortunately, through my network (my friend Christian is a font of local industry gossip) I heard about Sylvain, a young Frenchman with a glittering CV who had just come off the back of running one of the more progressive bakeries in town.

We met for a chat and seemed to see eye to eye on the exciting challenge of starting a bakery from scratch. I told him that quality was going to be the primary aim, and creating a warm, supportive work environment was at the top of my agenda. We would be ambitious and look to be one of the most exciting bakeries in a town full of them, but this might take time.

Sylvain was coming from a workplace that boasted a fully temperature- and humidity-controlled production room, whereas ours was shabbily insulated and proved to be around 10 degrees cooler than the mothership. This meant all our existing recipes for doughs would have to be reassessed, as the proofing time would increase significantly. On some of the early days in the new bakery, the cardamom buns wouldn't be ready for the oven until after midday, a full six hours after their usual expected baking time. In a perfect world, we would have invested in a proofing cabinet that could control all the relevant factors overnight to ensure things were ready to roll in the morning. In the meantime, we had to make do with hacks such as a small humidifier and electric heater – and it pays at times like this to have somebody with experience in your team who can take the initiative with adaptations and modifications and still achieve excellent results.

At the time of writing, we now provide the two cafés with our own sourdough buns (around 80 a day). We don't yet make laminated dough, so we buy frozen croissants in from another bakery and proof and bake them every morning. We're able to push out more of our bestsellers, so we have a good quantity of cardamom buns, cinnamon swirls and banana bread every day. We make and portion cookie dough and scones that we send to the mothership to be baked.

Upcoming investments include a laminator, which will enable us to produce our own croissants, pains au chocolat and more, and speed up the production of cardamom buns. A proofing cabinet will help ensure consistency of the pastries, especially as we take on new and less experienced staff, and as we start to ramp up production and take on potential wholesale customers. A final piece to add to the bakery would be a small deck oven so we can start to produce loaves in-house as well. There are some great micro-bakery ovens on the market (Rofco) and a new British-made model has been causing quite a stir – the Rackmaster 2020 by Campbell, of Wickford in Essex.

My approach to the bakery follows my now-established formula – start off small and build – while fully accepting its inherent limitations. This allows us to add pieces and invest in improvements gradually, getting to know our space and requirements thoroughly in order to avoid jumping into hasty purchases. While it's fair to say we've made a few bad calls and misjudgements along the way, their impact has been limited by their generally small scale. Breaking up the development of the business into small steps this way might appear frustratingly time-consuming, but it provides the kind of flexibility and agility that allows you to keep things on track as you work towards the bigger picture.

6 THE CUP OF COFFEE

Water; espresso; milk coffee, steaming and latte art; filters; iced coffee; cold brew; origins, processes and characteristics; resting after roasting.

Here we are then finally, the heart of the book! Obviously, this chapter will not be able to cover absolutely everything in the world of coffee brewing. It is, after all, a constantly evolving and changing environment, with new technologies and techniques coming along seemingly every few months. I will attempt here to cover the main topics

1. Espresso
2. Milk-based coffees
3. Filter coffees – batch and hand brew
4. Cold coffees

with a little theory, but mostly practical advice based on my own experience of learning how to be a (decent) barista and now trainer. How useful this chapter is will depend largely on your own experience with coffee brewing, but I feel that it's good practice, however accomplished you are, to revisit the basic skills periodically, and I often pick up something new when going over the simplest techniques with my team.

BUT FIRST, WATER

Before we consider the matter of brewing coffee, you need to have a think about your water supply. With overly soft or hard water, the coffee that you buy will simply not translate as it should to the cup: it will taste flat or bitter, and will be a long way from the tasting notes the roaster promised on the packaging. At the extreme end (and certainly in Copenhagen, where the water is extremely hard) you will encounter problems with limescale building up in your equipment within a matter of weeks if you don't treat your water effectively.

Somewhat ironically, I actually had a simpler time figuring out the water issue with the portable festival-style set-up I used during the early coffee cart and basement days. I bought water in 19-litre bottles from a commercial supplier, checking that it was at the right mineral balance of around 100ppm (that is, 100 parts per million of the different minerals that you find in water – have a look at the back of a bottle), which I would use for the espresso machine and filter coffee, with an empty bottle for the waste. This was only sustainable for a short period, partly because of the cost – around £12 per bottle – and partly because of the huge problem of storage. Blue plastic water containers around the bar have no aesthetic appeal. Thirdly, as we became busier with more customers sitting in, it became impractical to have to keep an eye on waste water levels – and there were definitely a couple of occasions on which the waste bottle overflowed.

When we became a little more established – 'grown up, like a real café', I used to say – the time came to look for a more permanent answer to our water problems. A contact in the industry told me about a company called Best Water Technology (BWT) which specialises in water solutions for both domestic and commercial environments across Europe. They visited to look at our space and we talked about what we needed – an effective way to produce the best water for both espresso and filter brewing. Due to the state of the tap water in Copenhagen, they recommended an RO (reverse osmosis) system. This is essentially a two-part filter that works by stripping the water down to what is essentially a zero state (also not good for brewing coffee – or for drinking neat, for that matter) and then *re*mineralising it to a level that is good to work with.

The *good* part about this system is that it is very effective at producing a stable water that is perfect for brewing coffee with, and you can control how much you would like the water to be remineralised (lower ppm water for filter, slightly higher for espresso: some ultra-perfectionist coffee shops use both, but we compromise with a setting that we find works for all our brews).

The *bad* news is that it is a rather large unit compared to a standard filter (it takes up almost a whole section under our bar) and it is rather expensive – and the expenses keep coming as you need to replace the remineralisation cartridge. As with most things, there is a middle ground which allows you to access this solution without the need to buy it outright. We essentially rent the set-up from BWT, who came to do the installation, are on call whenever there is an issue (not so frequently, but it happens), and change the filters. They also supply a separate filter in the back for the dishwasher and another one for the ice machine to protect them from limescale (yes, lots of filters).

Depending on your water supply (you can check the mineral content and overall state of your water with a bunch of different kits available online) and depending on how your coffee shop is going to approach coffee, this level of filtration might not be necessary. But it is definitely worth seeking expert advice from your local water company and your coffee roasters before running any water through your shiny new equipment.

Further reading
Water for Coffee by Maxwell Colonna-Dashwood

Now we've sorted the water out, we can finally get to the coffee!

ESPRESSO

We will start with the fundamentals. Espresso is quite literally the foundation of most of the drinks you will be serving, from Americanos to iced lattes, and it is here everything can go wrong or get off to a strong, balanced start. For this reason, it is one of the key ways to check whether a coffee shop has got its head in the game and actually cares about what is being served – *is their espresso tasty?*

Before taking your squeaky clean (and dry) portafilter over to your grinder, I would advocate weighing the portafilter and taring the scales (that is, setting to zero with the portafilter sitting on the scales) so you can get an accurate reading of the coffee your grinder spits out. There are some grinders on the market now that will do this for you (which can save valuable seconds – and believe me, these seconds add up on a busy shift) but otherwise you just have to get into the right habit until it becomes second nature.

The ground coffee goes into what is known as a *basket*. Now, it seems crazy, but not all baskets are made equally. When you zoom in close, the holes in a basket can be shockingly rough and uneven, which will have a knock-on effect on the extraction you achieve, and therefore on the flavour of your espresso. Remember, these small details add up, and you can taste the difference when too many details have been overlooked. One company stands out when it comes to baskets: VST have been producing their precision baskets for years now and most baristas worth their salt swear by them. So do yourself – and your customers – a favour and invest in a pair (around £35 each). The basket question is not over! Stay with me. Now you need to think about the size of the basket you want to work with in your coffee shop. These range from 15g all the way up to 23g at the larger end. I would recommend settling in the middle for the 18g size. This will have consequences for the recipe and ratio you will work with, which we will come to soon.

Next, you need to *distribute* the coffee evenly in your 18g VST basket. This means that you don't just work with the small mound the grinder has dumped in your basket, but you even it out before you tamp it down. A good distribution will reduce the risk of channels developing which will attract the water flow through the ground coffee and skew the extraction. We are looking for as even as possible a flow of the water through the coffee in our hunt for a consistently well-extracted shot. It probably won't surprise you that there are now a few tools that can help you take this to the next level, but to start with I would recommend practising the 'karate chop' – a series of light knocks with the side of your hand on either side of the basket to settle the coffee down in a nice, even, flat bed.

The next step – and here I do recommend investing in some equip-ment – is *tamping*. This is the process of applying pressure to the now evenly distributed coffee to create a compact, flat bed for the water to flow through in the next step. You can do this the old-school way with your hand, wrist and tamper working together to apply pressure. However, doing this 200 times a day (or even 50 times if you are not used to it) can be extremely taxing, and regardless of the attrition, it is very difficult to maintain a consistent level of pressure – a problem compounded if you have a team of three or four baristas working through the day, each one having a different physical make-up. The PUQpress was launched in the Netherlands in 2011 and has become a big hit in coffee shops all over the world. Essentially, this device does the tamping for you, with its flat tamp pushing down on your coffee with a consistent but adjustable pressure. If you want to reduce the errors that can happen when tamping – one of the most frustrating ways to mess up a shot – and reduce the physical demands on your team, then do make the investment in a PUQpress (around £800). Just don't forget to keep it clean...

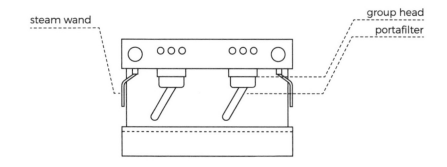

Next, you need to *backflush* your espresso machine to ensure no old coffee is clinging to the shower screen and to make sure the temperature of the *group head* – the component you lock the portafilter into to receive the pressurised hot water – is where you want it to be. Once the portafilter is locked in (fairly tight but not excessively so) you are ready to pull your shot of espresso. Make sure you have a cup ready underneath, positioned accurately to catch your stream(s) of beautiful coffee – you have no idea how many shots I witness (and yes, some are mine) that miss their mark and flow frustratingly onto the rim of the cup and down the side...

If you are using scales, don't forget to have them ready and zeroed/tared to the weight of the empty cup. I would suggest as a starting recipe to get a balanced and tasty shot that will also work well with milk, you go with a 1–2 ratio, that is one part dry coffee to two parts wet. So if you start with 18g of coffee in your 18g basket, look to get 36g of coffee in the cup. As you experiment with different coffees, different origins and so on, you may want to adjust this recipe and work with a longer extraction. It's very hard to give guidance on the time the shot should run, but in my experience you will never be too far away from a tasty espresso with a shot that takes around 23–27 seconds.

So the basic/starting recipe is

18g in -> 36g out in a time of 23–27 seconds

Americano (& Long Black)
A quick note on Americanos – which are simply espressos that are diluted with hot water, creating a larger, weaker drink. While we (and

many other specialist coffee shops) don't list it on our menu, we do get asked about it.[1] We recommend people who want to drink their coffee black try our batch-brewed filter of the day (see below) and we might even give them a small taster to convince them. But if they want a black coffee they can add milk to, and the day's batch brew is light or otherwise unsuitable for milk, then perhaps an Americano will be a better option. If you choose to serve these, the key is to avoid over-diluting by pouring too much water on the espresso. I would thoroughly recommend testing what you are serving before selling it. If you don't think it's good enough, then don't sell it!

The long black can mean different things to different people, depending on where you are in the world. For me, it's simplest to understand as a stronger Americano, which means less diluted and so less water. For others, it can all be about the order in which the water and espresso are mixed, so again, if you plan to feature this on your menu, make sure you test the various techniques and decide for yourself which one has the edge in terms of taste. The lack of an industry standard for these simple drinks is the perfect precursor to the next section.

MILK-BASED COFFEES

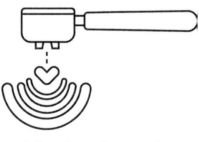

There are, annoyingly, many different names for milky coffees (it can be hard to keep up) and very little common understanding of what they entail. In recent years, coffees with names such as a 'magic' or 'Gibraltar' have emerged from around the world to join the ranks of the more seasoned flat whites, lattes and cappuccinos, in an apparent effort to confuse as much as anything else. By the time this book is in your hands there will probably be an additional four names to contend with. By and large, all we are talking about with these different names is the ratio of steamed milk

---

1 This isn't just some snobby, pretentious coffee place thing (I would argue). The thinking is that the baristas have dialled in the espresso to taste at its best drunk black, or perhaps with milk. By diluting it with more water, you are weakening the strength of the beverage and messing with its extraction. Some coffee bars, such as Colonna in Bath, offer a longer shot, or lungo, to give guests the bigger drink they might want, stronger than a filter brew and still dialled in on the extraction by the barista.

to espresso coffee. In an effort to keep things simple, we will stick to four classics:

Cortado/Piccolo

The smallest proportion of milk to coffee ratio – usually in the realms of a 50/50 split. Steamed milk with a little texture poured over espresso, perhaps with some simple latte art.

Flat White

The next size up when it comes to the proportion of milk. Hailing from the Antipodean coffee world, this drink is usually around 6oz in total, consisting of a double shot of espresso followed by carefully textured milk and latte art.

Cappuccino

This can look very different depending on where you are in the world, and what kind of coffee shop you're in. For some, it is a foamy milk drink with chocolate powder either sprinkled on top or mixed into the liquid. For others (and I include Darcy's Kaffe here) it's simply a more milky version of the flat white. We serve these in an 8oz cup.

Latte

For most people, this is the coffee drink with the highest ratio of milk to coffee. We still serve it with a double espresso shot (but some latte drinkers will ask for a single) and we use the largest of our cups (around 10oz), with a lighter milk in terms of fat percentage.

Milk steaming and pouring is probably one of the most crucial technical skills for a barista. After all, this is where you will be able to amaze your customers with beautifully presented latte art (see below how to create this). It's not the be-all and end-all of coffee brewing if you can't pour an inverted swan or perfect rosetta. But it is definitely part of the show – the theatre of the coffee shop, if you like – and there has been research to indicate that latte art can affect the perceived quality of a beverage, so it's well worth putting in some practice to get the basics right.[2]

---

2 'Latte Art Influences both the Expected and Rated Value of Milk-Based Coffee Drinks', Van Doorn, Colonna-Dashwood, Hudd-Baillie, Spence, 2015.

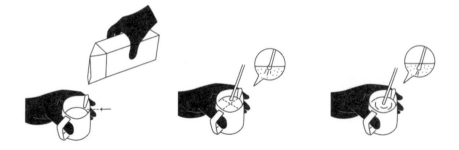

The Steps

1. Select a clean milk pitcher of the correct[3] size for your drink(s).
2. Pour the correct[4] amount of (ideally) cold milk/milk alternative into the pitcher.
3. Purge the steam wand on your espresso machine by flicking the power on and off quickly.
4. Place the steam wand inside the pitcher, roughly in the middle.
5. Switch the power on and then almost immediately bring the wand towards the surface until you hear a hissing sound.
6. At this point you will see the milk volume increasing, as you are now 'stretching' the milk by introducing air.
7. After a few seconds, when the desired volume of foam has been created, lower the wand back into the milk, slightly off-centre and begin to move in a circular motion to create a vortex effect – this smooths out the milk and reduces any bubbles that have formed.
8. Now it is key to get the temperature right. By holding the bottom/side of the pitcher throughout the process you can get a feel of how hot the milk is. We're looking to heat the milk to around 60°C and not beyond 65°C. This is the point at which the fats in the milk start to break down which changes the taste of the milk irrevocably.
9. Most baristas know they have reached this temperature a couple of seconds *after* the pitcher becomes uncomfortable to hold. It is a good idea to use a thermometer or temperature strip to check until you build up a good feel for it.
10. After turning the steam off and removing the wand, wipe the wand straight away and purge it to make sure there is no milk left.

---

3 See the image and page 75 for more on this. By industry convention, coffee cups are always measured in fluid ounces (oz), although I use metric measurements for everything else.
4 The minimum is to the bottom of the spout, the maximum is not much above the spout. Again, check you're using the correct size pitcher.

11. Swirl the pitcher a couple of times and tap it down gently on the bar to ensure the milk is integrated and to remove any last bubbles. The milk will start to resemble glossy white paint and you are ready to pour onto your freshly brewed espresso[5].

Pouring

Before starting the pour, make sure you swirl the cup of espresso thoroughly and quickly

1. Begin from a height around 8cm above the coffee cup, which you are holding at an angle facing towards you.
2. Once the milk hits the espresso, start mixing the two evenly and building up a nice base (the 'canvas') by pouring in circles.
3. Keep the speed reasonably fast and make sure that any white spots from the foam are eliminated by pouring over them.
4. As the cup starts to fill up, start to move closer to the cup with the pitcher or alternatively stop pouring briefly.
5. As you begin to pour very close to the espresso, making sure you are centred to the cup, you will see the creamy white foam begin to appear. Begin to straighten up the angle of the cup.
6. What you do now will determine what latte art you will create. Simply holding the pitcher in position as you straighten the cup and then pulling the pitcher through the cup will create a heart pattern; breaking the pour, starting again and repeating this process, followed by pulling through, will create a tulip. What you do here takes practice and research. Check out the videos of the YouTubers listed on page 78 and get practising.

---

5 There is a theory that espresso needs to be used as soon as it is ready and that it will spoil if left for even a moment. This is simply not the case and, so long as the cup used is warmed in advance, the temperature of the coffee will drop very little while you prepare the milk. It actually helps your pour to let the *crema* die down a little before starting, which will make mixing the milk and espresso easier to achieve.

How to practise

If you are new to latte art and need a way to practise without doing so on your paying customers and without using up too much of your valuable stock, there are some simple ways to do this. One thing we do with new team members who do not feel at all confident with milk steaming and pouring is get them to steam washing-up liquid to make chocolate and soap cappuccinos – mmmmm, sounds weird, but the results are so believable that I almost had Julia, one of our lovely (and trusting) chefs, drinking what she thought was a perfectly made coffee.

The process is simple and follows almost the same steps as above. Take the correct size pitcher for your cup (see below under Splitting). Put a tiny amount of washing-up liquid in the bottom and enough cold water to represent the milk in the jug. Steam away. You'll notice the foaming will be pretty full-on so, as with milk, try to get into the 'vortex' as soon as possible to avoid creating too much foam.

To create an espresso substitute, use chocolate powder combined with a small quantity of hot water (aim for the same volume as your actual espresso to create an accurate simulation). Then proceed to pour the well-swirled and integrated 'milk' over the 'espresso' as outlined above.

In order to keep up this practice flow, simply pour the whole cup back into the jug, then pour an espresso volume of the mixture back into the cup, sprinkle a bit more chocolate powder on top and then repeat. Depending on your chocolate/foam concoction, you should be able to do this loop a few times before it dies. The cups won't necessarily all look perfect. The key is to keep repeating again and again until the steps feel more fluid and you gain confidence. Try to concentrate on what you're doing and the results you achieve. It might be an idea to get a friend or colleague to film you. Then you can try to correct the mistakes on the next round and start to see visible improvements. Once this process begins to feel more solid, natural even, it's time to get the real stuff out and experiment with coffee and milk. Remember the fundamentals, keep the basic steps the same every time. Repeatability and consistency is the goal.

STEAMING AHEAD

Splitting

Over the course of my training and work, I've come to the realisation that one of the main skills that separates a proper barista from someone who can simply make a decent cup of coffee is the ability to split drinks – or more specifically, split milk between drinks. This is probably the same ability that separates a coffee shop that can keep up the pace when it gets super-busy from one that can't help but fall behind when a queue begins to form, or where quality drops a notch or two when the volume picks up.

The principles of making one flat white as opposed to four at the same time are essentially the same. It's simply a matter of scale. The *key* thing is to make sure you know what you can do with your selection of milk pitchers – and it may be worth investing in a few more sizes if there are gaps in the line-up. We have jugs all the way from 7oz (tiny and very useful for avoiding wastage on cortado orders or individual flat whites) up to 32oz (usually used for multiple takeaway latte groups). We know which jug to grab for '3xcappuccino', or for '1xcap', '1xfw', '1xcortado', for that matter. Maths can help with these calculations, but nothing beats good ol' trial and error for me.

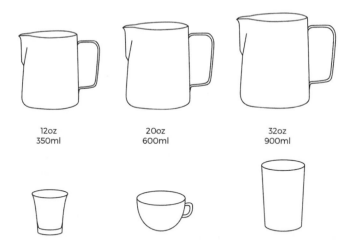

12oz
350ml

20oz
600ml

32oz
900ml

The next step is to start looking ahead, trying to work out which drinks *from separate orders* can be combined, thus saving time. There are a couple of things to consider here. One of which is your POS where drinks are ordered. For this to work smoothly, you need a system that is easy to read and organise. We used to mess around with handwritten paper dockets but the mixed quality of the penmanship was too much a negative factor (mine being the most 'doctorly' by far). If you do go down this old-school route, make sure you establish an easy to comprehend shorthand that new staff can pick up quickly; otherwise there will be missed orders and (potentially) tears – we used to dub a cappuccino with oat milk a 'Truman' (points if you can work that one out). We recently switched to a tablet system that allows us to carry out live edits (useful if people change their order or move table) and see the current waiting time (sometimes scary but very useful). This makes it a lot easier to organise the order in which we make drinks.

Which brings me to the second important point: the order in which the drinks are made. If you stick to the exact sequence of the orders you receive, regardless of whether they are takeaways or sit-ins, it will be impossible to combine drinks, and if it's busy this will slow you down. At the other end of the spectrum, customers can get irritated if they see drinks being handed over to people who clearly ordered after them. The key here is to get the balance right. Our current waiting time feature allows us to be more accurate with this, but remember that you're trying to weigh up people's expectations and avoid disappointing them. If a sit-in table ordered drinks together with food (and especially if they are a larger group of three or more), the chances are that they will be happy to wait a few minutes for their hot drinks, given that they will be chatting and maybe sipping the water you have provided them with. Takeaway customers generally expect to get their order more quickly, and I would rather they leave the space anyway so we don't have too many people hovering around the entrance or the bar. We take a name, or failing that a precise description, so we don't waste too much time finding them or, worse, give the coffee to the wrong customer and end up having to do a remake. *As always, a remake is the slowest option.*

Another factor to consider here is the number of choices on your menu, especially with dairy alternatives. I'm all for having options for my guests, whatever their requirements (something I learnt from Henrik – see Chapter 3), but the more choices on the menu, the longer orders will take – first, as customers umm and ahh at the cornucopia you have offered them, and secondly, to carry out as your opportunities to combine and split will be reduced. More choice also means more storage, and possibly more wastage if half-used cartons of almond milk have to be thrown out.

Lastly, the technical aspect of splitting milk. Once you have worked out the correct amount of liquid in the pitcher, it's important to get enough air into it as early as possible and stretch out the milk for longer – after all, you'll need enough foam for all the drinks you are making. Once you have steamed, grab another (clean) pitcher and heat it briefly using the steam wand. This is to ensure the milk doesn't drop too much in temperature during splitting. Then pour most of the milk into the new pitcher, leaving enough for the first drink in the original pitcher. (I always pour a little back from the second pitcher as I feel like it's easy to take too much on the first decant.) When you've done that, give the 'mother pitcher' a final swirl or two, then you are ready to pour. Once the first drink is out of the way, proceed to pour back some liquid from the baby pitcher to the mother. And again, pour a little back (perhaps it's my superstition). Then keep this up until all the drinks are poured. If you feel that you are running out of liquid or foam, you'll have to decide whether to risk trying to pour it, or quickly steam some more fresh milk. But only through practice and trial and error will you get confident with this and be able to breeze your way through busy days on the bar.

A final point here: make sure you communicate clearly with your front-of-house team to ensure they know which drinks you are making and deliver the right order to the right customer – otherwise all your complex calculations will have been for nothing.

Latte Art
Beyond the basics mentioned above (the heart and tulip), I won't attempt to describe more advanced techniques here. I'm no competition latte artist, and there are people much better placed and more talented in this department than me who can help push your patterns further (see the next-level baristas below). In addition, I don't think a book is the best medium for explaining the intricacies of pouring a seahorse or a rabbit. That said, I believe that everything stems from these simplified forms. If you can master steaming and pouring absolutely consistent hearts or tulips

across different drinks, in different sized cups and under pressure, then a) you've cracked the most important skills to be a good barista, and b) you are ready to take on more advanced pours if you feel that is something you want to explore.

Damon, the lead barista at Nostos in Battersea, constantly wows customers with his skilful pours (cue countless Instagram stories), but he does not do this at the sacrifice of other parts of his job (engaging with customers, taking orders, team communications and so on) and he definitely picks his moments – so nothing fancy when there's a queue during the morning rush.

If you want to check out some next-level baristas who are pretty good at showing how they pour, look for the following on YouTube:
- ❤ Lance Hendrick
- ❤ Morgan Eckroth
- ❤ Seven Miles Coffee Roasters
- ❤ Emilee Bryant

Automation

A final thing to mention on the topic of milk in coffee is the fairly new development of automated solutions that may be of interest to the potential coffee shop owner, depending on concept. Super-high-volume coffee shops have recently been exploring the use of tools such as the Übermilk, a device that provides the barista with temperature- and texture-perfect milk at the touch of a button (up to 250 drinks per hour). This can help the busiest of bars to keep up with demand for milk beverages, because as Colin Harmon explains in his book *What I Know About Running Coffee Shops*, the steaming of milk is always the biggest stumbling block in the flow of a beleaguered bar. While adding a device like the Übermilk can definitely help with this issue, you've also got to ensure your team can handle different milk options (potentially at least three), as well as times when the Übermilk might be temporarily down (I have seen many bars struggle when their understaffed baristas have to cope while the device reboots or enters a rogue cleaning mode).

Another recent addition to this market is the Wally Milk by La Marzocco. You still need to pour the milk into a jug yourself, but then the Wally will make sure it's steamed to perfection (you can set the temperature and texture levels). This takes away one potential source of human error from the bar, but it doesn't necessarily lead to quicker results. While baristas will not need to be as proficient at the steaming of milk, they will still need to be trained in splitting and pouring to ensure speed and quality in the beverages produced.

For me, neither of these options is the complete silver bullet solution for quality and speed with milk-based coffees. I also have to mention the cost of these options – circa £5,000 each – means they are not necessarily feasible for some operators.

FILTER COFFEE

Filter coffee – or drip coffee, as the Americans put it straightforwardly – consists of hot water being poured over coffee grounds and drawn by the force of gravity through a filter. Usually this is done through a paper of some kind, making sure the coffee oils and other undesirable bits don't make it through, but essentially the key difference between this and espresso brewing is the absence of pressure. As a result, it is a much slower way of making coffee – take your 25-second shot and multiply that by a factor of at least 10 – but the selling points of this method are manifold (quite beyond the simplicity of the equipment required).

First of all, the taste. Preparing coffee this way can produce a much more balanced and approachable cup than an espresso or an Americano. It can also reveal nuances and subtleties of the coffee that brewing with pressure struggles to produce.

Secondly, and perhaps most significantly to the business side of things, with filter coffee it's possible to make many more cups of coffee at the same time, while still producing high-quality drinks. You can effectively scale up your operation. It is just as easy (actually, it's easier) to brew a large batch of filter coffee on a batch brewer than it is to make 10 cups of coffee via the espresso machine.

Batch Brew

As with espresso brewing, the starting point to making good filter coffee is to work with ratios in mind. Here, the starting ratio is 60g of coffee to 1 litre of water, which will produce roughly 900ml of coffee (4 cups or so, depending on your cup size).

If you want to produce more or less, simply adjust the amounts based on this ratio. A half-litre brew will need 30g of coffee and a 2-litre batch calls for 120g of coffee. I use a free app to help me with this (my maths is awful – especially when I'm in a rush on the bar) called RatioCalc: you just plug in your starting ratio and adjust accordingly. The total amount you can brew will be determined by the size of your machine, but most can handle from around half a litre up to 2 litres. Make sure you check this before deciding which machine is right for you. We've outgrown two different machines and now work with a model from Fetco that allows us to brew up to 3 litres at a time and keeps the coffee (in a thermal carafe) hot enough to serve for as long as we need.

A word of warning about batch brewing. It may be tempting to brew a massive batch of coffee before opening and keep on serving it as long as it stays hot (which can be several hours). However, temperature is not the only factor that needs to be considered when it comes to a good cup of coffee. Freshness is also key. As the coffee sits in the thermal carafe and interacts with air, it goes through a process of oxidation which slowly robs it of its distinctive qualities and renders it flat and uninteresting. In our shops, we limit the lifespan of our batches to one hour after brewing. Much as we hate wasting coffee, we really do not want to serve a paying customer a substandard cup. If there is any coffee left in the pot after the hour mark, we will give it to the kitchen team or our neighbouring shops. If you find you are ending the hour with too much leftover coffee, simply reduce the size of the batch you are brewing, adjusting the quantities as discussed above. You'll get a feel for how much coffee you need to brew through the day over time. For example, we won't brew a large batch in the afternoon a couple of hours from closing; we will make a half batch.

Establishing a good balance between convenience (having enough coffee to survive a rush), freshness (how long the coffee has been sitting) and waste (not having to throw out too much) is the key to successful batch brewing.

Hand Brews

As beautifully simple as batch brewing is – and it is possible to get some fantastically good coffee from it – there is definitely still a case to be made for having other, more manual, filter coffee options on the menu. While the batch brew option is mainly about convenience, brewing coffee by hand is a more artisanal coffee experience and signifies that this coffee shop cares about what it's doing. This is the main point of the hand-brew menu for me: it allows us to showcase more of the coffee world. So we generally select an easy-going coffee for the batch, then one or two rarer, funkier, juicier (possibly more expensive) coffees for the hand-brew options, offering the customer a real choice. You have to be careful though – it doesn't make sense to offer individual hand brews as an option if you're not able to put the time and care into dialling them in properly, making sure that staff are trained to do so, having some key pieces of kit, and communicating to the customers what you are serving and why. And there's no point in putting hand brews on the menu if nobody orders them, and the beans and equipment begin to stale and gather dust. Likewise, if your shop is too busy and you cannot afford to spare a staff member to spend five minutes or so dedicated to producing just one or two cups, then it simply doesn't make sense.

There are multiple different hand-brew options that can work well for you in a commercial setting (V60, Kalita, AeroPress, Clever Dripper, Origami, Orea, April, Tricolate, Chemex to name just a few), each of which offer something slightly different in terms of techniques and final results in the cup. I won't go into all of these differences here; what I will say is that it is important to select a hand-brew option that works for you not just in terms of the coffee it produces, but also in terms of the workflow at your bar. For example, I would recommend looking at a quicker and less involved brewer such as the AeroPress or Orea if space is tight and you are going to be busy with lots of other drinks. On the other hand, if you can spare a barista and you have the space for it, the theatricality of brewing with a syphon can be an appealing option which attracts high levels of curiosity and engagement from customers. Again, think carefully how complicated you want to make the techniques and workflow, because it's key that training is provided for all staff members. Tetsuya, the current head of coffee at Darcy's Kaffe, trained for six months on Hario V60 brewing before he was ready to serve customers at Onibus in Tokyo.

A final comment on filter options is they are a bit of a compromise but can work well for high-volume bars that still want to serve a wide selection of coffees. There are automated brewers that mimic the techniques of brewing by hand (pulsing, circular pours that can produce a similar agitation/turbulence) while allowing the barista to continue other tasks. One such example is the Marco SP9 that allows the busy baristas at Prufrock and Rosslyn in London to keep pumping out the flat whites that dominate their dockets, while still offering a more rarefied coffee experience to the filter drinker.

OUR HAND-BREW TECHNIQUE

While it would be impossible to cover all the different hand-brewing options listed in this chapter (and each of these also has multiple techniques), I will briefly discuss the choice of dripper and the method we use at Darcy's Kaffes.

I have worked with Hario V60 (a pretty ubiquitous conical brewer with paper filters) since the beginning, partly because of my familiarity with using it at home and on busy bars. I find the paper filter much easier to work with than some of its competitors (Kalita 'wave' papers I find rather fiddly and sometimes slow) and combined with a simple brewing method inspired by James Hoffmann's technique, I manage to get great results across many different, contrasting coffees.

1.   Make sure you have enough hot water in your pouring kettle to rinse the paper and make your brew(s).

2.   Thoroughly rinse the paper with hot water to get rid of any papery taste that might affect the coffee. Dump this water.

3.   Grind the coffee, making sure to season the burrs with the coffee being used, and grind a little more coffee than you need to brew with (the grinder will retain some and you don't want to be tapping the grinder and getting fines, the coffee dust which can distort the flavour).

4.   Pour the coffee into the paper and make sure you have the desired weight (we normally brew with 15–16g).

5.   Tap and shake the brewer briefly to ensure the coffee is evenly distributed and check the water is at the desired temperature (we usually brew between 90–98°C).

6.   Begin to pour the water over the coffee at a fast rate, until you reach 50g. Swirl the brewer fairly aggressively to ensure the coffee is evenly saturated. Aim to do this in under 10 seconds.

7.   After 30 seconds, begin to pour using a circular motion, starting in the centre and moving towards the outside, clockwise. Pour up to 150g in 20 seconds.

8.   The last pour starts at 1 minute 15 seconds using a similar motion and finishing at 250g weight in total. Lift the brewer and swirl twice, followed by a tap downwards.

9.   Total brewing time depends on the coffee and the grind size but should roughly be around 3 minutes. After the brew is finished, we stir the coffee to mix it, then have a tiny taste to ensure the coffee is good (and is the right coffee!). Coffee bed should be flat and even, with no coffee on the sides of the paper.

10.   Serve to the customer and perhaps pour a little into their cup, explaining the coffee a little and that its taste will develop as it cools down.

This is the template for our pour-overs, but the details of grind size, water temperature and coffee weight depend on which coffee we have selected and how it is tasting. We generally brew naturally processed coffee at lower temperatures, funky coffees with a slightly lower dose, and clean washed coffees at higher temperatures. These decisions will all depend on what you are looking for in terms of taste, so what you need to do is get testing and track the results of different variables. This is the fun part!

COLD COFFEES
Iced Coffee

The biggest seller for us in the summer is iced coffee. There are a few different iced coffee drinks that we offer, but by far the most popular (and probably the simplest to make) is the ice or iced latte. This is simply a decent quantity of ice (we use a 12oz takeaway clear cup – our biggest) topped with milk of the guest's choice, leaving enough space for the espresso to be poured on top. If you're careful about this stage and you pour slowly onto the ice cubes, the espresso will hover on the top of the milk and look pretty seductive. Then the customer can stir the drink to mix the components together before drinking. If you want to serve the beverage ready to drink, then you can swirl or stir it before handing it over. This looks less cool but will taste better. One more option is to steam the milk and the espresso together briefly, both to mix them properly and to create a little texture. Then you can pour over ice into the glass.

It's important to bear in mind that with ice lattes in particular, people might want the addition of sugar. There is something about cold espresso and unsteamed milk that can highlight the bitterness in a coffee, so I would say that adding a little sugar syrup here is not a crime against coffee (it's an ice latte after all!). In cold coffee season (always expanding – blame climate change? – but roughly April to October in Denmark), we keep a simple syrup made with a 1:1 ratio of water to sugar in a squeezy bottle in our bar fridge ready to be added to a shot of espresso. We don't offer any other flavoured syrups with our drinks, as we like to allow the coffees we have selected to be tasted unadulterated, but depending on your location you may have to consider this option. I know from personal experience that most London cafés tend to offer the full gamut of nut flavourings, usually by way of the trusty Monin bottles, and in the US, people like things extra-sweet. I will just make two comments: think about how complicated you want to make your menu, and the added time it will take guests to make up their minds and place an order; secondly, *keep those bottles clean!* The number of times I have seen syrups being poured into drinks from filthy bottles is frightening – and I'll never forget reading a review of a café that pumped crystallised flies into ice lattes . . .

SIMPLE SUGAR SYRUP RECIPE

1. You're going to work with equal parts of sugar and water. Let's say 500g of sugar to 500ml of water.
2. Heat the water and sugar together in a pan or pour hot water from the coffee machine over the sugar in a milk jug.
3. Stir until the sugar is fully dissolved, then allow to cool.
4. Pour into a squeezy bottle and then make sure to date it. (It should last in the fridge for up to a month.)

There are plenty of other options for cold coffees but we always like to serve a really good no-milk version. We have found that increasingly customers are veering away from chugging gallons of either milk or alternatives in both hot and cold coffee drinks. Personally, I don't always find a creamy ice latte really hits the spot in terms of refreshment. So in season we make daily batches of filter coffee designed to be served and consumed cold. There are a number of ways this can be done, from brewing with hot water over ice for a quick chill to cooling the coffee down by placing it in the freezer to blast it (remember to transfer it to the fridge before it freezes). We choose a coffee that we feel will taste good cold, perhaps a juicy Kenyan or a fruit-forward Colombian or even a delicate, peachy Ethiopian. We will then brew it in our Fetco batch brewer, upping the proportion of coffee a little and grinding it slightly finer than usual to produce a more concentrated beverage. This will balance out when poured over ice, which dilutes the liquid as it melts. So our standard 120g>2-litre brew will turn into 130g>2 litres, ground two lines finer on the EK43. Every coffee is different so please do this by taste to get the best out of the beans you're using. In general terms, you're looking for a juicy, vibrant brew that refreshes with perhaps a hint of acidity. Our regular batch brew will be more *comfy* than this profile, so we're going up a notch.

Anyone for C&T?

Tonic-based cold coffee drinks are a great option in the summer. While the espresso tonic has been around for a number of years (as far as I'm aware, the lovely people at Koppi in Sweden created it – they certainly serve a fantastic version), it is still relatively unknown in the wider consumer world and is definitely not something you see on the high street. It is relatively simple to make: you need a good, fruity, ideally lighter-roasted espresso (Kenyan works well, or a fruity Colombian), ice, a good tonic (we use Fever-Tree's Mediterranean) and maybe a garnish such as a lemon twist or grapefruit slice. As in presenting an ice latte, pour the tonic over the ice first (we use 100ml – half a small bottle) then carefully pour the espresso over the ice cubes so it hangs in suspension, making a beautiful-looking drink. Then serve to the guest with a stirrer or straw, explaining that the drink should be sipped to taste the espresso on top, then mixed to enjoy fully.

Cold Brew

Another option for cold black coffee production is cold brew. This is a more lengthy process but can produce a huge volume of coffee in one go, which I have found useful for summer events away from the café. You need a bit of kit in order to brew the coffee and then strain it thoroughly. The brand Toddy are cold-brew specialists and their kits are available in a range of sizes and all around the world, although you can definitely put together your own set. I find cold brew tends to flatten a coffee somewhat, so you might lose the delicacy of a washed Ethiopian or the singing acidity of a Kenyan, whereas the more funky naturally processed coffees can retain their profile well.

One of the best cold brews I have tasted was at Anana Coffee/Food in Athens. The co-founder, Christos Giachos, is a genius at brewing all kinds of coffee but the cold brewing in particular was impressive. He had selected a Brazilian naturally processed coffee that retained its fruity richness and sweetness when cold brewed.

The basic principles are: place coarsely ground coffee (think French press levels) in the bottom of your vessel; pour filtered water in a ratio of 1 litre to 60g coffee carefully over the ground coffee, making sure it's evenly covered; give the coffee a stir to make sure everything is saturated; then simply leave the container (room temperature is fine) for at least 12 hours and up to 24 before straining it and chilling it in the fridge.

One nice way to use the cold brew is to decant it into small glass bottles (plastic if you have to) that can be labelled and sold as a grab-and-go option. One summer I made some of these with a small amount of sugar syrup and oat milk, which proved popular. They should keep for a few days and still be good, but if in doubt, taste and decide for yourself before you serve them to paying guests.

TIME TO GIVE 'FRESH ROAST' A REST?

'Freshly roasted' used to be one of the standard slogans of quality coffee establishments (it still is in some quarters). But in the last few years, the conversation has moved towards a discussion about resting coffee – which allows the gases imparted during the roasting process to dissipate. This shift has followed the rise of lighter-roasted coffee, originating in Scandinavia with roasters such as Tim Wendelboe (Oslo), Coffee Collective (Copenhagen) and Koppi (Helsingborg), but now happening from the US (Sey) to Japan (Onibus). Due to their roast level, the beans in these coffees are denser than darker roasts and hence take longer to de-gas.

We've enjoyed some of our best-tasting espressos and filters several months after the roast date. A coffee from Honduras roasted by Sey comes to mind that we accidentally 'lost' and then brewed after finding it four months later. We had struggled initially with a batch of the same coffee three weeks after roast, but this time around it was incredibly clean, complex and moreish, and a lot more *open* than before. Theory tested and proven, as far as I'm concerned. Try it yourself!

Obviously, resting coffee might be a luxury that not all coffee shops can afford – they simply might not have the space to store it. But do your best to find a solution for this so you're not tearing the latest delivery box of coffee open and pouring it straight into the hopper. Some roasters will even store and send rested roasts out to you. As long as you're not using old-school dark roasts, you and your customers will really taste the difference. In terms of storage, a cool dark place with low humidity is best, and once you open a bag, try to store it in an air-free environment (push the air out of a bag before sealing, or use an Airscape canister – they are simple and work well).

COFFEE ORIGINS, PROCESSES & CHARACTERISTICS – A BRIEF GUIDE

This is no more than a rough outline of the most common coffee origins and processes, and their general characteristics. It would be impossible here to provide an exhaustive guide, so I'll recommend some other literature that offers a deeper dive into this topic. We try to get the staff at the Kaffes to the point where they can all talk in general terms to a guest about different coffees, so they can recommend a retail bag or offer advice on the choice between filter and espresso options.

In (*very*) general terms, coffees from **African** producing countries (Ethiopia, Kenya, Burundi, Rwanda, DRC etc) are fruity and with degrees of acidity. Ethiopia is the birthplace of coffee, where arabica plants grow wild.

Coffees from **Central and South America** (Brazil, Colombia, Peru, Costa Rica, Ecuador, El Salvador, Guatemala etc) tend to be more comfortable options, with a sweeter and rounder profile. However, there is a *lot* of variety within the region, with Colombian coffees in particular offering a huge spectrum of flavour because of the country's terroir and experimental producers.

More unusual to see in the west, but becoming increasingly visible, are high-quality coffees from **Asia** (China, Thailand, Myanmar etc). These tend to be heavy and sweet with low acidity. Indonesia, especially the island of Java, has lost its historical pre-eminence as a producer, while Vietnam is the world's biggest producer of robusta coffee beans, used in commercial blends.

It is worth repeating again that these are the most general characteristics possible, and there is a world of nuances out there to explore. One big factor in this is varietals – the specific variety of arabica coffee bean will of course have a factor in the taste, depending on where it is grown. The second one is processing.

COFFEE PROCESSES

Knowledge about coffee processing (what producers do with the coffee after it is harvested) is increasingly crucial as the development of this side of the industry has sped up inordinately in the last few years. Until recently, there were really only a couple of processes (washed and natural) that you would see on coffee bags, but that has now expanded into myriad variations and experimentations. Again, any attempt at providing a comprehensive guide would add another 50 pages (at least) to this book, but I will give the broad outlines as well as recommend further reading and listening.

Washed

This is one of the main foundational processes for the industry and most good-quality coffee has traditionally been processed this way to preserve the characteristics of the original bean. It is a 'light touch' approach that still involves fermentation (all coffee is fermented in some way), but essentially the seed is removed from its surrounding flesh and the coffee is washed with clean water. Other than that, there can be other variables that will affect the intensity of flavour but you can expect a washed coffee to be clean, clear and crisp in its profile, with potentially higher acidity than other processes.

Darcy's partner Scarlett Hessian helping to map out the basement layout.

Scarlett miming the coffee machine, trying to figure out the layout of the basement bar.

The first bar.

Darcy making coffee in the early days of the basement.

Serving Callum in the early days of the basement café.

The basement café in all its glory.

Darcy, happy as Larry in the basement café.

Darcy (left) and André, trying to look jovial outside Rantzausgade.

The exterior of Darcy's Kaffe on Rantzausgade, Copenhagen.

Darcy Kaffe's Covid takeaway menu, modelled by Scarlett.

Darcy's Kaffe on Rantzausgade, busy again after the lockdown was lifted.

Getting busy in the Rantzausgade branch.

Darcy in the Carlsberg pop-up shop.

The exterior of the Carlsberg pop-up shop.

Carmen behind the bar at the Frederiksberg branch. Carmen was the first manager of Darcy's Kaffe and a frequent collaborator.

The exterior of the Frederiksberg café.

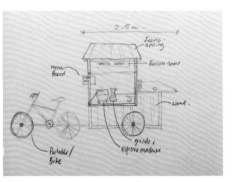

An early sketch, by Scarlett, of our mobile coffee cart.

The first event that kicked things off. Joined by Scarlett.

Market day with the mobile set up.

Piping berliners with rose-and-rhubarb jam.

Gooseberry brioches, with André.

Preparing the day's fresh sando.

Piping berliners with elderflower custard, with André.

The staple: BMO—bun, butter, cheese.

'I owe this person a lot.' (Darcy's partner Scarlett.)

Scarlett and Sandy, posing like architects.

Scarlett and Sandy, working late on the
espresso renovation.

'This shot still makes my heart flutter.'

Natural

This is the other process that you are most likely to see. It refers to the coffee being dried (and fermented) in cherry – that is, inside the fruit. This will generally give the coffee a heavier profile, potentially sweeter or jammier. We tend to love Ethiopian naturals, particularly tasty on espresso and with a bit of milk. Like a pudding!

Honey

This is one of my favourite processes. The bean is removed from the cherry but left with a layer of mucilage on as it dries, giving the coffee a sweeter and smoother profile. You might also see a colour attributed to the process (yellow, black, red etc) which refers to the amount of mucilage left on; this is most common from producers in Costa Rica but is also used elsewhere.

Anaerobic

In general terms, this signifies that the coffee has been kept in an environment free of oxygen, often in a sealed tank with a one-way valve. As the coffee ferments, carbon dioxide and other gases are given off, pushing the oxygen out of the tank. This process can help cultivate yeasts and bacteria that may push the flavour profile of the coffee, while reducing microbes that may spoil the coffee and also reducing oxidation. Among other variations, you can get both washed and natural versions of this approach, resulting in vastly different taste profiles.

Carbonic Maceration

Similar to the anaerobic approach, but this involves flushing the tank of coffee with carbon dioxide in a technique borrowed from wine making. In Beaujolais, the grapes are fermented in this environment whole – i.e., inside their skins – and this is also true of the coffee: it is fermented 'in cherry'. Done well, this process can help push the fruitiness, acidity and intensity of flavour in the coffee, creating some unique or unexpected flavours.

Among these main processes, there are many variations and emerging processes that continue to push the industry. Depending on your café, your guests and the suppliers you work with, it may be interesting to look further into experimental processes such as thermal shock, lactic and koji (see resources for more on these).

GOOD COFFEE-MAKING HYGIENE

Knowing how to make good coffee is one thing, but working as a good barista involves more than just what goes into the cup. The way you work is also key: stay clean, organised and structured.

- Keep the cloths you need for the day separated, neat and clean. One cloth *just* for cleaning the stem wand, one/two for the drip tray of the espresso machine, one for touching up cups in case of espresso drips etc, and a couple for bar surfaces (depending on the size of the bar). I like to use colour-coordinated microfibre cloths for these tasks, but find the cloth that works best for you.
- Keep a small brush on hand for cleaning the areas around the grinders and scales.
- Always flush, always brush. Get into good routines. Flush the group before every brew (rinsing them and ensuring the heat) and constantly brush and wipe your surfaces to work clean.
- Aim to clean espresso machine group heads and backflush groups periodically during the day, and particularly after busy rushes. (See resources for more on this.)
- Establish a clear end-of-day cleaning procedure for your equipment to ensure consistency across the whole team.
- Keep an eye on your equipment and make sure that you have a good coffee machine mechanic on call in case of emergencies. For example, grinder burrs might need to be changed every few years, depending on usage and volumes. Consider writing a log to keep this process manageable.
- Remember to empty the hoppers of coffee into a sealed bag or box overnight. A full hopper left overnight is often a signifier of how serious a shop is about their coffee. How can you clean a grinder that still has beans in it?

7 MORE THAN COFFEE

Other drinks, hot or cold; food to buy in or prep yourself – sandwiches, banana bread, *bolle med ost*.

A successful café these days needs to offer more than just great coffee and service to complete and compete. What you can and should offer in terms of food and other drinks very much depends on the location and spatial limitations of your shop (is there adequate space to have a kitchen? Can you install an extractor? And so on) so analysing your choices is the first step towards determining the extended menu. Ask yourself if it is a place where people will linger and sit to eat, or more of a grab-and-go set-up. What is the local competition? Getting this part right will help your business get the most from its transactions, maximising spend per customer – you should aim to give each customer at least the choice of buying one more item in addition to their cup of coffee. I try not to see this as a purely numbers-driven business decision, though – it's more a matter of offering a better service to guests, of giving them what they want.

HOT DRINKS
Tea
In the UK (traditionally a land of tea drinkers, if increasingly turning towards coffee) it's imperative to have a decent tea selection, no matter how focused on the stronger stuff your coffee shop is. The days of having the best flat whites in the area and a choice of beans for filter but then simply offering PG Tips or the equivalent for the tea drinkers are over. Why would you serve tea drinkers, or those who have maxed out their day's coffee intake, something ordinary while pouring beautiful cups for the rest of your guests? (Could it be a misplaced sense of pride in being a *specialty coffee shop*?) More importantly for your business, why would you make people choose between paying a visit to your café or to the one down the road that has a better selection? There's *always* going to be a tea drinker in a group.

You don't *have* to go down the artisanal loose-leaf route, though. After all, it might not make sense for a high-volume, predominantly takeaway site. Although it is possible to pre-weigh loose tea leaves yourself into disposable sachets (and this might well end up being the most cost-effective approach), there are plenty of companies out there doing a fine job of making decent tea affordable and pre-packed in bags for wholesale convenience (such as Good & Proper in the UK). At Darcy's Kaffe we have been working with Postcard Teas of London and Companion Tea of Berlin for a number of years now. These companies only source the finest teas from small-scale producers, and since most of our tea drinkers are staying in we're able to offer them a pot which we refill up to three or even four times for some of the green teas. We charge a higher price than for standard tea, but hopefully it's an experience that guests will remember and come back for.

Key things to consider with teas are convenience vs quality; correct brewing techniques (green teas generally brew at lower temperatures etc); the option of matcha tea (or similar – we use a ground oolong from Postcard); and herbal teas such as lemon verbena and chamomile (both big sellers at Darcy's Kaffes).

Chocolate and more

A good hot chocolate is imperative. It's popular in the winter, for kids and adults alike. We use a powder by Mörk, a company with roots in Australia but also based in the EU. It offers four grades of strength and we find the 'junior' level (50 per cent cacao) works best: 20g powder, 200g milk, quick whisk then steam and pour. In the depths of winter we get through so many bigger portions that we have considered making a pre-mixed liquid that we can simply pour in a pitcher and steam, as it is the measuring and whisking that takes time. And remember, every second counts in a busy coffee shop. While we are in a rush, we can't skip the whisking phase or there will be dry patches of powder in the final beverage and an understrength and weak drink.

Remember this when you're busy: if people are waiting for a little while and they receive a well-made drink in a considerate and friendly manner, they will forgive and forget the time they had to wait for it. If they wait, but then get a badly made drink, sloppily presented and in a rushed manner, that waiting time (even if marginally shorter) will stand out. *Make it worth the wait.*

Hot toddies and ginger shots are also great to offer in the colder months, when it seems that everyone around you is getting sick. While you can buy pre-made drinks to heat up for convenience, it is pretty easy and more cost effective (plus charming) to make something yourself by heating lemon, ginger, honey and water, infusing for a while, cooling and then bottling. Or you can make a base that you then dilute and steam on the coffee machine for a few moments.

Here's the thing: coffee machines have multiple uses beyond the steaming of milks of different kinds. In a pinch, they can be used for heating a range of beverages from mulled wine/gløgg to hot toddies and even just water. I've used my event machine to heat up some soup when we were getting behind on service (those big soup warmers can take an age to heat!). There's even the possibility of making scrambled eggs with your steam wand (check out James Hoffmann's YouTube video for more on this topic). I recently discovered that this is fairly standard procedure in Paris after hearing what I thought was some questionable milk steaming. Just remember to give the steam wand a good wipe down, purge and soak afterwards – as you always do anyway.

COLD DRINKS

We always try to keep the fridge on display by the counter fully stocked with a really nice selection of bottled drinks, from orange and apple juices by a local company using waste fruits (Twist:D) to unsweetened iced teas, a few quality sodas (Karma Cola and their ginger beer and lemonade) and sparkling water in glass bottles. We also work with a local company, Table Ferments, that provides us with wonderful kombucha (a fermented and naturally bubbly tea-based drink) made fresh and delivered once a week. We make our own seasonal soda (elderflower & rose, strawberry & pink pepper), although we find it difficult to keep up the supply of quality homemade drinks in the summer. We try to strike a balance between homemade and niche commercial brands, and we've steered clear of multinational corporations such as Coke because they are available in every convenience store and supermarket – we need to maintain our points of difference.

We haven't gone down the route of producing smoothies and juices in-house as we figured that it didn't really work for us. These kinds of drinks involve equipment (decent commercial blenders and juicers don't come cheap), space and staff that I didn't feel that we would be able to provide. It's more important to me to be serving good hand-brew coffees than in-house smoothies. Another café with a different emphasis might make a different call: if your menu is more focused on brunch and food than showcasing top-shelf coffees, the investment in staffing, machinery and so on could be worth your while. Just remember, you will need to have a good fruit/veg supplier to keep well stocked – and that juicing and blending create noise levels that may not be acceptable.

Another quick point about drinks that we don't offer but which can add value to a café: a selection of alcoholic drinks on the menu will definitely add another revenue stream, especially if you are planning to extend your opening hours into the evening. But it is not necessarily easily done. Having wine/beer/cocktails on the menu seems perfectly normal in cafés in southern Europe, but the ease with which you can transition from a coffee shop to a bar very much depends on the licensing laws that apply in your location. The possible exception to this is serving wine at private out-of-hours events (see Chapter 8).

FOOD

There is a wide range of possibilities for what you can offer in terms of food, from the most basic selection of pastries and snacks up to restaurant-level cooking. A lot depends on finding the balance that suits you, your site, your budget and your customers. I am by no means a chef, but I know from personal experience that it is possible to provide a basic breakfast and lunch, even in a tight space. The way I see it, you want to reduce the number of choices for the potential guest. It used to be in Copenhagen that you could go to one place for a good coffee which might only have pastries to eat, but if you wanted a proper breakfast or a bite for lunch you would then go somewhere else. I wanted to create a place that would take this decision-making away so you could get both under one roof. As mentioned in Chapter 1, I travelled to Australia and New Zealand when I was younger, where you would find neighbourhood cafés everywhere that served up decent (and often much more elevated) brunch dishes alongside friendly hospitality and *proper, well-made* coffee. Later, when I was living in London, I would see places opening with roots in this Antipodean style (think Bill's or Kaffeine in particular, avocado on toast in general). I sought out these places on trips to Berlin, Amsterdam and Paris.

Think about your offer: can people drop in to have not just a good cup of coffee, but breakfast, a decent bite for lunch or an afternoon treat? Even with limited space and equipment you can still offer overnight oats, instant porridge pots and toasties in addition to pastries and biscuits – anything that can be prepped ahead (perhaps when you're closed) and keeps well. There's a good reason why banana bread is on the menu at almost every café you visit (see banana bread recipe on p. 99). Also, think of using day-old croissants as toasties: sliced open and filled with cheese and ham (we've even put kimchi in ours), they are delicious. This way you are avoiding waste by turning it into a key ingredient for the next day's tasty snack. We offer soft-boiled eggs at the cafés, boiled ahead of time, quickly cooled and then either kept warm in a sous-vide or quickly reheated with hot water from the coffee machine or kettle. This is an easy hack but there are shortcuts for poaching, too.

In terms of equipment, you don't need to invest in a lot to get your kitchen off the ground. A toastie press is a good start (the more expensive ones designed for commercial use will last longer and toast better, but a decent domestic model will do to get things going); an induction plate (Ikea has a cheap and cheerful one); a small oven (our first was so tiny it could only accommodate three croissants at a time); a few chopping boards; a cooling rack; and a few pans and knives. Once business picked up, we invested in a food processor, a bigger and better oven, a water bath or sous-vide, and eventually a Thermomix for ultimate prepping flexibility.

The Menu

You will need to find a menu that suits your business, but from a fairly early point we had established the basic outlines of our line-up and 'concept'. We decided to keep it simple for ourselves by offering only one sandwich option for lunch. However, we made sure it was something special and a little bit different to what you might find anywhere else – and it would change almost daily (this last part was a challenge and we no longer change the sandwich quite so often). We would usually make it vegetarian to minimise the number of guests unable to consume it (fortunately for us, Copenhagen has a surprisingly low number of vegans or people with intolerances to certain ingredients).

Keeping it so simple – almost spartan – meant that we didn't need to keep stocks of ingredients which would take up valuable space in our small fridge (we started with a second-hand domestic one) and would potentially spoil and be wasted if not used (it always caught me by surprise how busy we would get). At the same time, limiting the choice in this way meant that we could really nail a tasty and interesting sandwich that would be by default seasonal, dynamic and 'only available for a short time' – a nice sales pitch that possibly added to the 'hype' of our offering. We would always prep a small number of these sandos together and have a little stack on display at the same time every day (11 a.m. – Danes lunch early). This meant that we had a solid grab-and-go option that allowed people to swing by during short lunch breaks or with illegitimate car parking (the wardens in the area are notoriously swift on their bicycles). A tantalising display that oozes instant gratification goes a long way to sell a dish (have you ever been to an Ottolenghi café?).

Alongside this solitary lunch offering, we would have some pastries – generally a mix of those bought in from local bakeries (we are blessed with many good options: a shout out to those we worked with – Alice, Met, Democratic, Il Buco, Andersen & Maillard and Brød) and some of our own creations. Remember the laughably small oven I mentioned that we started with? Well, André, our master baker (or 'chief concept culinary chef' – CCCC – as we dubbed him), would come up with daily bakes such as croissants stuffed with cream, citrus jam and marzipan made with various seeds and then re-baked, in a brilliant reboot of the standard almond croissant (he suffers from a severe almond allergy). Or he would knock out some simple yet stellar brioche buns with various toppings and fillings. These looked, smelt and I'm sure tasted (we would produce in such small quantities that we had to sell all we made and forgo our hard-earned quality control duties) absolutely amazing, and complemented our 'dynamic' sandwich menu, so we soon developed an expanding crew of regulars for our food, as well as the coffee that was our initial focus. The news of our interesting café-fare travelled as far as the upper echelons of fine-dining Copenhagen, attracting visits from no less than René Redzepi of Noma and Rasmus Kofoed of Geranium (successively World's Best Restaurant in 2021 and 2022), as well as regular patronage from chefs, bakers and food bloggers.

Over time, we have expanded the menu slightly. During the Covid lockdowns when we were reduced to performing as a takeaway venue, we scrapped the fresh sandwiches for a time and went instead with toasties – toasted sandwiches, paninis or whatever, two slices of bread filled and grilled. This meant we could reduce the quantity of perishable ingredients needed and prep more in advance, thus reducing pressure on an increasingly stretched staff. The strictest periods of lockdown coincided with the coldest months, so a warming sandwich offered welcome comfort to those on their little ventures out into the strange landscape of distanced public space. When we were able to open up again with inside seating (how amazingly odd that felt!), the toasties had proven so popular we had to keep them in the regular line-up alongside our fresh sando. As the kitchen facilities and team grew, we added a seasonal salad and soup, and while we still offer only one version of each item, we now have three options at lunch, which enables us to cater for most moods.

At the weekend we aim to have a 'special' dish that involves slightly more intricate prepping and plating. This allows us to hype up the weekend a bit more and ensure there is a demand for booking tables (see p. 115 for more on this). This kind of cooking also motivates our kitchen team, as they are called on to create new dishes and have an input on the menu. This is also definitely part of the reason why talented and experienced chefs apply to work with us.

THE SANDO

Our basic formula is to think in layers: start with an interesting spread on the bottom, then the 'meat' of the sandwich, followed by some nice salad leaves and interesting pickles. We have played around with using standard sourdough bread, baguettes and a kind of ciabatta sourdough long bun, and have found that something with a crust on both sides, such as foccaccia, is the winner as it doesn't get soggy and is easier to eat. Classic baguettes have the tendency to get a little too crunchy and hard on the gums...

Combination Number 1
Baked onion cream cheese + charred padron peppers + pea-shoot salad + pickled fennel + grated Gammel Knas cheese (aged Havarti)

Combination Number 2
Lime, coriander and spring onion mayo + Szechuan-spiced baked aubergine + sesame pickled carrots + hard cheese such as pecorino

> The key for us is to mix it up and keep it interesting, both for our guests and for ourselves. Having a few tasty pickles and sauces in your arsenal is super-useful to add quick pops of flavour and interest to what is a simple and humble dish.

Finding A Good Bakery Supplier

Unless you plan to open with a full-scale in-house bakery, you will need to find a good-quality and reliable supplier for your baked goods, from morning pastries to bread for toasties and sandwiches. Depending on your location, there might be a plethora of options or you might struggle to find even one. Either way, you need to test the product selection before deciding, figure out the logistics (who is delivering and when), and work out whether the costs work for your menu. In bigger cities with lots of dedicated wholesale bakeries, the pastries are baked and delivered through the night, which might make for ease of logistics, but means that by morning some pastries will be far from fresh so you'll start the day with drying-out goods.

With your bread supplier it's important to figure out how you will be using the loaves. If you are using bread predominantly to make toasties, then it's better that the bread is left to dry out a little before being used so it toasts more efficiently. One of our first bread suppliers (a celebrated bakery) supplied us with loaves whose crust would burn to charcoal black when toasted on the second day. So run some tests before making a final decision. Another option might be that you get the bread delivered pre-sliced. This is perfect for assembling fresh sandwiches or prepping a batch of toasties, but be warned that the exposed slices won't stay fresh for long.

In the beginning we combined baking our own special items and a couple of staples with pastries delivered fresh from local bakeries. We didn't make a great margin on these (20 per cent at most) but we used them as a lure to attract butter-hungry customers in the morning. What's a more classic combo than a morning coffee and a buttery, flaky croissant?

Two Staples: Banana Bread, Bun & Cheese

One item that we started to produce ourselves early on and that hasn't left the menu ever since (around three years and counting – like a West End or Broadway production) is our banana bread. This may not seem at all innovative but there is a reason – there are several, in fact – why banana bread is such a popular item to serve in coffee shops all over the world. These include: it's relatively easy to knock out; it's pretty cost effective as the basic recipe doesn't involve expensive core ingredients such as chocolate or nuts; and people love it throughout the day from opening to closing time. It's the perfect, slightly naughty sweet item that can always be justified (it's relatively healthy; it's only bread with some added fruit, after all). It's also something that can be easily customised to different palates and dietary requirements. A top-notch café I recently visited in Paris had four different versions, including chocolate, nuts and gluten-free/vegan. Our version was initially adapted from Felicity Cloake's recipe in *The Guardian* (itself an adaptation of recipes from other cooks), and has since become our own signature. Below you'll find our current recipe – feel free to try it out for yourself but I would encourage you to use it as a springboard for your own version.

Miso Sesame Banana Bread

Ingredients (to make one 1.3kg loaf):

- 550g plain flour
- 45g sesame seeds
- 5tsp bicarbonate of soda
- 360g sugar
- 800g mashed banana
- 5 eggs
- 150g yoghurt
- 160g melted butter
- 75g miso (light)

Method:

1. Mix dry ingredients together, making sure to sift everything.
2. Combine wet ingredients thoroughly with mashed banana while slowly melting butter and miso together.
3. Pour wet ingredients into the bowl with the dry ingredients, mixing until there are no dry parts left.
4. Pour the melted butter and miso mix into the bowl last, giving everything a final thorough stir.
5. Pour into a loaf tin greased and lined with parchment paper.

6. Bake in a 160°C oven for an hour, and check loaf is done by inserting a skewer.

7. Leave to cool in tin before removing and slicing.

While banana bread is definitely a hero item with appeal around the world, in Denmark there is a savoury item that can't be ignored – a little culturally specific, but perhaps it could be transported elsewhere. The humble bun and cheese – *bolle med ost* (BMO) – is found everywhere around the country, and while they vary widely in quality, they're universally popular with both native Danes and anybody who has spent a significant amount of time there (when I'm away from Denmark, I find myself pining for them).

Basically, the snack consists of a bread bun, most likely made of sourdough these days, cut open and spread with butter (although this is optional) then filled with cheese. The choice of cheese of course varies and has a huge impact on the elevation of the bun. When I first arrived in Copenhagen and was a bun novice, thinly sliced Comté was the fashionable choice for the best buns in town. Nowadays, Arla Unika's Gammel Knas (an aged Havarti) has gained ascendancy around town and is our selection.

The great thing about the bun and cheese is that it offers a savoury snack for all times of the day that can double up as a quick meal for beleaguered mums with prams or people rushing to catch a train. You even see people in the rush hour bike lanes chomping on a bun as they cycle along, so clearly the format lends itself to convenient eating – outside Denmark, perhaps a close equivalent is the *onigiri* (rice balls or triangles)

sando

BMO

sold at railway stations in Japan. For a café, it's an ideal item to serve: super-easy to prep (we cut about 2.5kg of cheese a day), relatively cheap to produce and a guaranteed sell-out.

SPECIAL DIETS AND INTOLERANCES

It can be difficult for any hospitality business to cater for what seems to be a growing number of people with food intolerances or special diets. You should also remember that some – if not all – of these are dictated by medical necessity, so it is always counterproductive to regard a customer as simply fussy – which, of course, a paying customer has every right to be anyway. The kitchen should be particularly careful in the handling and labelling of nuts: for some people, the allergic reaction to even a tiny quantity of nuts can be disastrous, even fatal. So it is well worth thinking through ways of keeping your menu flexible, with vegan and gluten-free options, as well as keeping abreast of current trends in dairy alternatives.

8 DEALING WITH THE CUSTOMER

How to recruit and reward regulars;
put a lid on it; dealing with complaints;
coffee shop as workspace.

The single most important task for any coffee shop is to provide the customer with a reason to buy coffee from you. In most cases, customers can make coffee at home, or in their office, or they can buy it from another place down the road. So you need to ensure that the experience of buying a coffee from you is at the very least a pleasant one.

You also face the challenge of ensuring consistency on one hand, and individuality on the other. By consistency, I mean both consistency of product and consistency of service. There is a saying in the industry that 'you'll always be judged by your worst cup of coffee'.

Every single cup of coffee that you serve might be a cup that determines your standard in a customer's opinion: if it is not good, they will take their custom elsewhere next time, and they won't add their name to your roster of regulars. They might even tell their friends, even thousands of contacts on social media. So make it your duty to ensure that the very worst cup of coffee your shop serves is better than the standard offering served by your closest rival.

You might make a mean cup of coffee yourself, and you may have hired a rockstar barista whose coffees earn you a good name, but all the goodwill the pair of you have created can dissipate with one bad cup of coffee from your weakest link.

You can substitute the need for consistently good coffee with the need for consistently good service – so, by extension, your coffee shop is only as friendly or efficient as its worst-tempered, coldest and least efficient member of staff. One lapse, whether it is rudeness or forgetting a key element of an order, can have a fatal effect on a customer's judgement of your business, and can be difficult to retrieve.

Here, though, you need consistency with individuality, rather than the robotic consistency of 'Have a nice day' delivered with a fixed smile and glazed expression. We make it a policy at Darcy's Kaffe that there has to be some sort of verbal exchange with every customer who comes in, to show that we care about them, that we are attending to them while they are our guest and are interested in what they have to say.

There are no particular rules about the subject of the exchange, although when in doubt it is best to stick to first principles and say something simple about the coffee they are about to drink: its origin, where it was roasted, its flavour profile, anything particularly interesting or unusual about it. The customer's response will usually give a clue about their level of interest and whether or not they would like to know more.

There's also a judgement to be made about how far to take the conversation. On the one hand, the customer who is wearing a hoody and earphones is making it pretty clear that conversation is not really on the agenda – so don't push it. On the other hand, there is nothing more annoying to people waiting in a queue at a busy time than seeing the person at the till engaging in a long exchange with a regular or an old mate, stretching out a five-minute wait into ten minutes. So you need to find ways of politely ending a conversation and moving on to the next customer in this situation.

There are a couple of other things which I believe single out coffee shops and differentiate them from bars or restaurants. Firstly, people of all ages and any sex generally feel comfortable going to a coffee shop alone, simply to have a cup of coffee, whereas for other hospitality venues they tend to go by arrangement, in couples, pairs or groups.

Secondly, and especially at less busy times of the day, away from the morning or evening rush hours, customers often feel they can ask general advice from staff in a coffee shop in a way that they don't elsewhere. It's difficult to pinpoint exactly why, although it is a feeling I am familiar with myself when I visit a district or a city I don't know: bar or restaurant staff always seem somehow too preoccupied to help out, or they make it clear that they only work there and don't know the area, whereas we somehow assume that coffee shop staff are locals, are part of the community and will be able to point us in the right direction for whatever we want: the nearest post office, a good local restaurant or whatever.

One of the coffee shops I worked in before opening my own closed at the weekend because the owner actively discouraged tourists and out-of-towners, on the grounds that they come along just once, they want everything you can give service-wise, they are time-consuming, and they have a tendency to leave irrelevant but nevertheless possibly damaging negative reviews on social media. For my part, I have always taken the opposite view – perhaps, I suppose, because I still remember the reception I received as a foreigner in Copenhagen, and in particular the warmth of the welcome in coffee shops. So I am always ready to help out a visitor to the city and give them a few 'insider' tips and recommendations. Sometimes, this attitude pays immediate dividends: there is a hotel directly opposite Darcy's Kaffe on Rantzausgade and several groups staying there have 'discovered' us on their first day and made us a kind of base for their stay, returning every morning for breakfast and the chance to pick up some more information.

In most cases, of course, tourists will never come back, but I still believe that looking after them makes sound business sense. They may well have friends who will visit Copenhagen down the line, and they are often active on social media during their trip, offering potential free advertising – and if just one per cent of the tens of thousands of tourists who visit Copenhagen each year were to drop in at Darcy's Kaffe for a flat white, that would represent a big boost to our trade. This is not just wishful thinking: a large part of the appeal of Copenhagen in the past decade, along with its bicycle-friendly status and cool Scandi vibe, has been the food scene headed by two of the world's most famous restaurants, Noma and Geranium. And of course many foodies are eager to have a decent cup of coffee during their daytime pre-dinner tours of the city. Then there are the coffee tourists: serious coffee fans who will research online to find the best or most interesting half-dozen coffee shops to visit during their city break.

TO LID OR NOT TO LID

There's a question I insist on asking every customer who orders takeaway coffee: 'Would you like a lid?' In fact, it really annoys me when I order a coffee somewhere else and they automatically put a lid on. I happen to be one of those people who don't like lids. I like to see the surface of the coffee, and to breathe in its aroma – both the visual and the aroma contributing to my enjoyment of the drink. Other people have their own reasons for disliking lids; my father says he always burns his mouth or spills the coffee down his shirt when he attempts to drink through the spout in the lid. I also think it is wasteful to give lids to people who don't specifically want them, and there is already enough to feel guilty about with the use of disposable coffee cups.

However, I do think it is quite reasonable to offer lids to those who want them, for whatever reason: it might be quite a long walk back to their office, or to the seat in the park where they like to drink a still-hot coffee. And I also think it is part of the service for us to put the lid on for them: if we leave a pile of lids out for people to help themselves, there will be spills, lids touched by multiple hands, wrong sizes chosen and so on, all contributing to more wastage.

Even among regulars, there are several categories, and it is worth finding out where each one fits. There are some who come every day – even twice a day, morning and afternoon, bless them! – as part of their routine. They might live nearby and work from home, so treat your coffee shop as a little escape; they might work nearby and duck out of the office for lunch or a break; or they might find you a convenient stopping-off point on their commute between home and work. Whichever is the case, it is well worth the effort to find ways to 'reward' them without appearing to penalise or neglect other customers (see box on p. 111).

Then there is a group who might only come once a week, probably at the weekend. Theirs is a social and leisure visit, so they tend to linger longer and have more than one drink as well as the brunch that we cater for with an extended menu of specials. This group comes less frequently than the daily regulars, but they spend significantly more per visit so are equally valuable.

There is also a category of familiar visitors – we barely think of them as regulars – who might drop in twice a week or twice a month, depending on their schedule. They would probably come more often but we are not really on their route and they have to make a special journey. If we're lucky – and this has happened more than once – they move house or change job, and suddenly we see them every day.

RECRUITING MORE REGULARS

Coffee is a notably high-margin, low-cost industry. The mark-up per cup might be relatively high (see Chapter 12 on pricing), but a coffee shop has to sell a lot of cups of coffee to stay profitable. This is doable, and plenty of shops manage to thrive on takeaway coffee alone, hardly even bothering with nibbles to go with it and providing no seating or tables. But unless you happen to be right next door to a major tourist attraction or transport hub, you are unlikely to be able to reach your sales targets through passing trade or first-time customers alone. So it is of paramount importance to build a core following of regulars – the people who drop in throughout the year, whatever the season, and who keep you in business (although it goes without saying that everybody who crosses your threshold is a potential regular, so first-time visitors need to be treated with just as much courtesy and welcome as your best regulars).

With any luck, this core group of regulars will establish itself and grow organically: somebody drops in to your coffee shop, likes the coffee and the vibe, so they come back – again and again. But there's no point in just being passive and seeing what happens – you need to be active and do whatever you can to kick-start the process or recruit more regulars.

I will assume you conducted your research before even opening, the sociological stuff I studied at university: who lives and who works in the immediate vicinity, who passes nearby on a daily basis. Are any of these groups likely to be regular visitors to your coffee shop and, if so, how are you going to attract them?

In most cases, the answer will be by looking generous but acting smart. If you are near a university campus, the obvious move would be to attract students with discounts: students are notoriously broke, but they have a lot of time on their hands and like hanging out, so they can represent a good market. But you have to be judicious: do you want them to descend on your coffee shop in such numbers that your other customers feel swamped and stop coming? Also, it can be a risky strategy to make your business over-dependent on a demographic who disappear for months at a time during their long vacations.

Another group who came to the fore during the Covid-19 pandemic are health workers and first responders, who might be worth targeting if there is a hospital or health centre nearby. They work 52 weeks a year and your other customers are unlikely to feel aggrieved if you offer them generous discount deals.

You may be able to reach other groups in similar ways. Offering a discount directly to employees of Company A, simply because it employs 500 staff, may well be a turnoff to employees of Company B, which just has 12 staff – or, for that matter, to self-employed freelancers. But many large employers on the scale of Company A offer a package of staff benefits, such as membership of a local gym or subsidised deals at local restaurants and cafés, so it is well worth approaching the company to sound them out. In Copenhagen, there is a tradition in many offices of meeting up at a communal table on a Friday for pastries, which you can arrange to deliver. Other companies with their own coffee machines might welcome a weekly delivery of ground speciality coffee as a little luxury to share among staff.

HOW TO RETAIN THEIR AFFECTION

For some regulars, the deal is pretty straightforward: they just want to enjoy a good cup of coffee in a nice environment, so consistency and efficiency are the most important factors. Others, though, crave a bit of variety – they might be coffee aficionados, with a real interest in developing their knowledge and extending their appreciation of different styles, so they will respond happily to new or unusual beans from a range of sources and roasteries. They might also get bored and be tempted to wander elsewhere in search of better options if you fail to provide an attractive variety.

I think it is generally best to have a fairly neutral – but still high-quality – standard coffee on offer at all times: one that works well in milk-based coffees such as cappuccino, latte and flat white. It won't offend anybody who likes coffee, so will be the 'safe' option for casual walk-ins and first-time visitors. It could either be your own standard house blend, or you could vary your beans, but always within the 'safe' profile.

At the same time you could offer a rolling range of more distinctive, funkier coffees available as pour-overs to keep the connoisseurs among your regulars happy and stimulated – plus any drop-ins who identify themselves as interested in a more experimental approach. Some of the coffees available these days are a long way from standard – the taste profile of coffee is broader than that of wine – and the beans on the wilder shores can be pretty divisive: my brother took a bag of coffee home with him saying it was the best he had ever tasted, but his housemates all reckoned it was undrinkable. Also serving something controversial in the shop can open up interesting conversations and offer the chance of excellent PR: if you offer the customer a free alternative if they don't like what they have chosen, most will drink it happily but all will remember and appreciate your generosity and transparency.

This is just the sort of small gesture – not forced or scripted – that will make your coffee shop stand out and show that you really care about the customer's experience, the equivalent of the incremental improvements that push the cost of a bottle of champagne up from £20 to £100 or more.

As an owner-operator, I am always on the look-out for new ideas, new ways to improve what we offer – and I have the advantage over the chains that I can introduce them overnight. Every time I am being served – in a bar, a shop, on a flight – I am conducting research: there are always useful tips I can pick up or adapt.

PROBLEMS WITH REGULARS

Everything I have written so far about regulars paints them in a positive light and that is definitely how I see them. But there are one or two things to be wary of when dealing with this valuable crowd. Of course, we want everybody, especially regulars, to feel at home in our coffee shop, but some people can start to make themselves a little too much at home for your comfort.

In the early days of Darcy's Kaffe, I had no employees at all: the Kaffe was, quite literally, just me – every shift, seven days a week. So my early regulars enjoyed a very special, even exclusive, relationship with me. This state of affairs could not last indefinitely and my gradual recruitment of staff meant that I could have some necessary time off as well as spend time away from the bar doing other things that contributed to building up the business.

Most regulars understood this and welcomed it, forming good relationships with incoming staff and enjoying the development of the business and the improvements it brought, especially in the provision of food. One or two, though, couldn't help making me feel that I was somehow neglecting them by my absence. This type of person may also like to assert seniority over new staff members, as if they were somehow custodians of standards. It might be worth mentioning this to new staff recruits, to reassure them if there are some particularly troublesome long-term customers to deal with.

You should also remember that it is a straightforward human fact that many people like routine and are resistant to change – and many of us will have felt a pang of regret when a small, almost private 'discovery' where we could always grab a seat becomes more generally known and popular, to the point of being overcrowded at busy times. So don't take your long-time regulars for granted when you get busier – do your best to be as welcoming as you always were in the early days, when perhaps you needed them more than you do now.

THE INEVITABLE COMPLAINTS

Dealing with unhappy customers is a fact of life in any service industry. It always has been, as evidenced by the traditional saying that 'the customer is always right'. As anybody on my side of the bar knows only too well, this is simply not true: the customer can frequently be rude, ignorant, opinionated, misguided, prejudiced or simply in a bad mood; occasionally even a bit strange. Ramping up the pressure these days, social media can bring out the very worst in people, emboldening critics who would never have dared to complain to your face, either through shyness or because they know at some deeper level that they are in the wrong.

Some coffee shop owners are infuriated by criticisms they receive online and I know exactly how they feel: we recently received a so-so review for our morning bun and cheese offer from an amateur and completely non-influential blogger – and I can't express how disappointed I was, even though I know I should just shrug it off.

But in general, my attitude is to embrace the whole process – particularly with Google reviews, which are the most influential if only because they have the widest readership: they pop up automatically when you search out a restaurant, bar or coffee shop and they are the ones I look to when I am visiting a strange town. Yes, ridiculous and almost fictional complaints can feel unfair and frustrating, but the fact that it is being discussed on a public forum gives you the opportunity to show that you are being transparent and take an unsatisfied customer seriously – to show that you care. And at least negative feedback gives you the chance to correct whatever went wrong: in the days before social media, dissatisfied customers often just walked out, leaving the proprietor completely in the dark about what had gone wrong and therefore unable to correct any error that had been made.

In general, I try to react whenever I receive a notification of a review. If it is a good review, I thank the giver and look forward to seeing them again. If it is a bad review, I do my best to reply without over-reacting. If the complaint is not specific, I try to find out the details of what went wrong – and, bearing in mind that the exchange is in public, I try to be calm, respectful and gracious – to take the high ground. The alternative is to appear defensive or rather passive-aggressive, which is never a good look. After all, it is possible to lose more customers if you mishandle the situation.

If, having considered the matter carefully, it seems to me that the complaint is unwarranted, I will briefly but firmly explain my position, while apologising as graciously as I can for any inconvenience the customer suffered. If I believe they have reasonable grounds for the complaint, I will have words with my team. And if, as is so often the case, there has been a simple misunderstanding or unwitting mistake, I might offer the customer a coffee on the house next time they are passing. But I am careful not to move too quickly to this type of free offer, only making it once I know it will be an effective way of solving the situation – after all, I don't want to encourage that section of the community who delight in earning freebies by complaining.

It should go without saying that any social media I do on behalf of Darcy's Kaffe is part of my job – it is part of our branding, and must be done professionally. So it is always worth sitting on a complaint for a few hours, probably overnight, rather than reacting to it on a hair trigger, when emotion is running high. This will also give me the time to find out what happened from the perspective of my team. And with delicate matters like customer complaints, never respond when you are tired and possibly short-tempered at the end of a long day, or conversely, slightly disinhibited after winding down with a glass of wine and well up for a digital scrap. It's just not worth it!

And always remember the positive aspect of Google reviews. Yes, we'd love to have uniformly 5-star reviews, but given the nature of the business and the vagaries of coffee drinkers, a steady 4.6/4.7 is pretty good (and scores of 4.2 or less can be a useful sign that you are getting too many things wrong). Those high ratings mean you will pop up on maps more often, raising awareness and bringing more customers through your door. See Chapter 11 for more on the importance of these different platforms.

REWARDS & 'THE BOOK'

As soon as Darcy's Kaffe had settled into a routine and I found that I had recruited my first batch of regulars, I started thinking about how I could reward them for their custom – and encourage them to stay loyal.

Offering rewards is an issue which divides operators in the industry, with strong opinions both for and against. Historically, the big chains have adopted variations on the loyalty card, which can be used across various branches – originally a little card that the person manning the till would stamp, offering a free coffee when the purchaser reached 10 or 12 or 24, and more recently a credit-card-style plastic card.

Independent coffee shops often reject this approach for three reasons: one, that it smacks of the big chains, which is something we seek to avoid; two, that it devalues our product by making it look like we are overcharging in the first place; and three, because it is a nuisance for customers already suffering from card fatigue, who have to remember to carry yet another card around with them every day.

All these objections have their merits, but it still struck me as fair and logical as well as good business practice to reward our best regulars both financially – they are after all providing us with steady income – and emotionally, by offering them a form of recognition that shows we don't take them for granted.

The solution I came up with was to introduce a pre-pay system and what we grandly and slightly mysteriously call 'The Book'. It works very simply: the customer pays in advance for six cups of coffee and we write their name in an alphabetised address book we keep on the bar and put a tick beside their name each time they order one of their pre-paid coffees. Once they have six ticks against their name, we give them a seventh cup for free. In fact, it is an extremely generous reward, running at almost 15 per cent – far better than most loyalty cards that reward on a cumulative basis. So the argument that we are devaluing our core product may be stronger than ever – but I am still convinced it is worthwhile.

Set against rewards that kick in only *after* the customer has reached their 10th/12th/24th coffees, our reward system has the benefit for Darcy's Kaffe of payment up front and in advance – exactly the type of transaction every business wants. By pre-paying, customers are committing themselves to becoming regulars: if they have a choice of two coffee shops but in one of them there is a pre-paid coffee waiting to be ordered, this is the one they will choose. Pre-paying for 10 coffees might look a bit too expensive, and remind people of how much they are spending on their coffee habit, while receiving such a generous discount for just six – linked more or less to the days of the week – seems both a decent bargain and not too steep.

Furthermore, there is another psychological effect that was noted a few years ago, when some of the more expensive restaurants in London started selling 'tickets' to meals costing well over £100 a head. Everybody – including the restaurants themselves – expected the move to be deeply unpopular, but in fact diners rather liked having the stress of paying or dividing a bill taken away from them, and they appreciated the delayed gratification of paying for something and enjoying it the next month – rather like paying for a holiday in advance. Having already budgeted for the meal in the previous month, they were also more likely to splash out further on cocktails before the meal or a better-than-average bottle of wine with it – so both diner and patron were left happy. We have noticed a similar effect with pre-paid coffees, as regulars with advance coffees paid for and in The Book are more inclined than usual to splash out on a pastry or a slice of cake to accompany the drink.

There's more to it than that. There's something satisfyingly old-school about ticking off numbers in a physical book, as a respite from the wired world of click and collect, electronic payments and apps that we all live in. There's also something clubbish about it, and who doesn't want to be part of the in-crowd? Better still, it is a club you don't have to 'join': membership comes via the simple act of pre-paying for a few coffees.

The other clubbish aspect of The Book is that we don't advertise it, either on the written menu or via any of our social media. Membership is by informal invitation, in that we will ask somebody who shows signs of becoming a regular if they are interested. But there's nothing secretive or sly about it. If a customer sees it in action and asks if they can join, we always say yes: after all, they are in effect requesting permission to become regulars and why would we reject them?

The benefits for us don't end there. The Book is an easy way of getting to know our regulars by name and a ready index of the people we might invite for a glass of wine after hours on a special occasion, such as the anniversary of our opening. It is especially valuable to new employees, for whom it provides a crash course in identifying our regulars and putting names to their faces.

THE COFFEE SHOP AS A WORKSPACE

In recent years, a fault line has developed in coffee shops around the issue of work. The tech trio of laptop, internet and mobile phone has combined with the growth of freelancing and working from home to create a large new class of professionals who no longer spend their working hours cooped up in offices. Some of them work in home offices, but many don't have much space at home, they have noisy children or housemates, or they simply want a change from the four walls where they live. As a result, they look for an indoor public space where they can settle down with a laptop to work. The more scholarly may head for a public library, but they face competition from schoolkids and the elderly – and the threat of supervision by strict librarians. So a great many end up spending at least part of their day in a coffee shop.

This same crowd – primarily young urban professionals – is very much the coffee shop's core market. So we do well to cultivate them and welcome them into our premises. After all, we need steady trade all day, not just for breakfast and lunch, and who else is going to drop in for coffee at 10 a.m., 11 a.m., 3 p.m. and 4 p.m.? We also have to recognise that, given that we operate during working hours, many of our customers are on call if not actually working while they visit us. So answering a phone call or responding to texts and emails on their mobile phone is unavoidable.

It should be a matter of a simple trade-off: a seat at a table for the price of a cup of coffee. But the terms of trade are never clear: should ordering a coffee and a croissant entitle you to an hour's occupation of a seat at a table? What about the second hour? It never ceases to amaze me – and everybody I have discussed the issue with in the industry – how many customers think it is quite reasonable to sit on a single cup of coffee for three, four or even five hours while they take up space in the warmth of our precious premises – even through a crowded lunch hour.

But it's not simply a case of me being annoyed at having a reasonable crowd scattered around the coffee shop between 11 a.m. and 12 p.m., but only selling two cups of coffee. A coffee shop is – or should be – a communal space with a convivial, even buzzy atmosphere. That ambience is killed if a majority of the people in the room are not really present, but instead are plugged into earphones and attached to portable computers, tapping away at their keyboards in a work bubble. Some are shameless, taking part in loud Zoom meetings or long phone conversations, so everybody nearby has to endure hearing their contributions. I have even seen customers pull plugs out of sockets in order to plug in their laptops (one reason why some coffee shops have hidden sockets so they can operate a vacuum cleaner after closing).

So how do you set the parameters, should there be rules, and how do you police them? First of all, you need to determine what works best for you and your particular customer base. Some coffee shops welcome working freelancers unconditionally as an essential crowd in their district; others ban laptops completely. The worst solution, in my view, is to rely on customers to be reasonable or to vary your attitude depending on demand and time of day. This invariably ends up with conflict, or with you asking a customer to vacate their seat – neither of which is desirable. It is never pleasant to refuse service to a potential customer because they need to work, but I have seen pairs or groups who have arrived to have lunch together walk out when there was plenty of room for them because they did not want to be surrounded by silent workers – and that is the worst result of all.

At Darcy's Kaffe, we have taken a middle path which recognises that for some of our regular customers, working in a coffee shop at least part of the time is a necessity. So, in our Rantzausgade branch, we allow people to settle in and work at the 'worst' seats at the back of the premises, along with one table that can be booked for communal working and meetings. We also allow unrestricted access to wifi, acknowledging that this is now part of modern life even for those not working. Laptops are banned on all other tables – including all the most popular spots near the windows and in the corners. This demarcation is clearly signalled with small signs on the tables (which some customers are shamelessly happy to remove or hide from view so they can pretend ignorance) and our staff are alert to correcting infringements politely as soon as a laptop appears outside the designated area. In addition, laptops are banned completely at the weekend, when it tends to be busier and we endeavour to create a more social atmosphere for people to linger over brunch. We also have a booking system which allows a portion of the tables to be booked by groups. This gives us the ability to approach people who have been there for a long time and inform them (nicely) that we need the table back, and it also helps create a culture around the café that it is not 'just' a good work spot.

On the whole, this solution works and keeps everybody more or less happy.

9 STAFF AND CREATING A CULTURE

Hiring (and sometimes firing); roles and rules; pay and rewards; create a culture of 'making the effort'; finding the 'flow'.

In the early days, Darcy's Kaffe was just that: it was the cup of coffee that Darcy made for you. I worked solo, if only because I had no choice. After all, I had no budget, and no idea whether any customers would grace my basement, so the very concept of employing staff was beyond the bounds of possibility. And that's how it remained for months, even once I had established that – phew! – yes, there really was a market for my coffee. Darcy's Kaffe was only open when I was there to open it, which meant dragging myself out of bed before dawn on cold, wet winter mornings; doing all the 'extras' that are part and parcel of running a coffee shop, such as picking up supplies of coffee, milk and pastries either before or after hours; and working long hours six days a week – seven if I wanted to open on a Sunday or had a special event to cater for. I was permanently exhausted and aching from being on my feet all day, but fuelled by the excitement and the challenge of working for myself.

I had still not really considered staffing options when somebody I knew from a previous place I had worked at – a barista who was really into coffee and had kept in touch when I was doing pop-ups – suggested he could cover for me for a few hours if I needed a break. I jumped at the chance. Another customer, André impressed me with a video on Instagram demonstrating how to make a pour-over. He was also a skilled baker, and was soon doing pop-up sessions on a Saturday, when he would create incredible waffles with fillings he had concocted from foraged ingredients – they always sold out within a couple of hours. But both these guys already had jobs and I was in no position to ask them to quit in order to join me on a permanent basis.

This all changed when I opened a spin-off Darcy's Kaffe at the former Carlsberg factory development, five kilometres across town. I could not physically be in two places at once, so I hired Dan, the friend who had been filling in for me on an occasional basis, to run the new place. Now we were two – but more were needed when Carlsberg came to an end and the main Kaffe in Nørrebro moved from its cramped basement into a spacious corner site. Very quickly, it seemed, I had become an employer for the first time, and the issues that every employer faces became real to me.

The first of these issues that struck me is just how important the staff are, especially in a customer-facing business. Whoever is on duty on a chosen day becomes the face of the business to any customer who walks through the door. So your staff represent you in a very literal way and you need to be able to rely on them absolutely: you're in their hands. So it is of paramount importance to recruit with care.

The second big issue – and one that took me by surprise – is how quickly wages become the biggest single expense for a coffee shop (perhaps for many small businesses), accelerating past rent costs and the ongoing investment in equipment and supplies by the time you have assembled a small team. It is also fair to say that as a boss, a large chunk of your working time will be devoted to the multiple tasks involved in employing and managing staff, from interviewing and selecting individuals through to on-boarding, training and career development, plus the day-to-day management of shifts, of working combinations and human relations.

As befits my status as a complete novice start-up entrepreneur, I really had no idea if my business would ever expand, so when it did, all growth was organic and all my planning was reactive. There were no projections or flow charts, so I had no idea that I would employ one barista after three months, another two months later, and a cook at the six-month mark. By and large, I would take somebody on whenever we reached the point that we couldn't cope any more, or whenever a member of staff announced they were leaving. That's the system by which I still operate, and unless your business is on a much larger scale, it seems to me the most flexible option – and flexibility is the key: after all, I never know how long an individual will stay with us, and there's never an orderly turnover of one member of staff leaving every three months. Instead, Sod's Law dictates that three will announce their intention to quit on the same day. In an attempt to hedge against this scenario, though, I do make a point of responding to any promising-looking CVs that come in and keeping the details on file – and it is always useful to know of a couple of students who may be available to help out during busy periods during their summer vacation.

One advantage of this ad hoc approach to employment – only taking on staff when they are really needed – is that I have largely avoided every employer's worst nightmare: paying people good money to stand around doing very little. It's not that I am especially mean, or a particularly hard-driving taskmaster. But I genuinely believe it is my duty to keep my staff happy, and that they work best and get the most satisfaction and pleasure from their job when they are busy – not over-stretched and exhausted, but engaged in something they value and enjoy doing.

In general, I don't advertise when we need new staff at Darcy's Kaffes – I have never placed a paid ad or worked through a third-party recruiter, and only rarely have I even issued a call-out for staff on social media. I don't need to because every day I receive unsolicited applications from people looking for a job, and every week or so one of them will be outstanding, which means that I have more potentially good candidates than I can ever accommodate.

In many cases, I am flattered – sometimes almost embarrassed – by the calibre of the applicant. I receive messages from highly skilled baristas, coffee specialists and chefs who have visited Darcy's Kaffes as customers, and from some who have never set foot in Denmark but know us from our Instagram feeds. These applicants are responding to our serious focus on the best coffee we can find, sourced from interesting roasters in Copenhagen and beyond, combined with our general attitude of warmth and fun. Like me, they are ambitious, love coffee and want to enjoy their work.

In late 2022 a message landed from Lowdown, a well-known coffee shop in Edinburgh: Tetsuya Yamada, a brilliant barista who had trained at Onibus in Tokyo and had been working with Lowdown for a while, wanted to continue his European sojourn in Copenhagen; was there an opening at Darcy's Kaffe? I am always looking for ways to raise our coffee game, and offered Tetsuya a role as our Head of Coffee, which he was happy to accept. In March 2023, after a month of intensive after-hours training at our bar, he was narrowly beaten into second place in the Coffee Masters competition at the London Coffee Festival – one of the world's ultimate tests for professional baristas.

Most people – or at least, the sort of people I want to employ – are not primarily motivated by money. It is important to pay a decent wage, especially in an expensive city like Copenhagen, and I make a point of paying everyone for the hours they work – unlike some high-end restaurants, which are notorious for expecting people to work unpaid overtime. But I am not in a position to compete against high payers, and am happy to lose staff who only follow the money.

I firmly believe that if you provide a dynamic and passionate workplace that is fun to work in, and if your employees don't feel exploited, then they will be engaged and fulfilled. It follows from this that any effort you put into looking after your team will be rewarded – not just because it is the right thing to do, but because it will help to generate the happy atmosphere that attracts both customers and staff. Word travels fast in the world of hospitality, and your good name as an employer is incredibly valuable.

There are some in the industry – Rosslyn in London, for example – who recruit for attitude alone, on the basis that they can teach skills. This is a laudable, even enviable, approach to staffing, but perhaps you need a bigger establishment than mine to make it work. From the outset, if I needed baristas, they had to know already how to knock out a good cup of coffee – I really didn't have the time or space to teach the basic skills. That said, seeing Starbucks on a CV will not fill me with confidence: the mass-market way of doing things can be very different from what is expected in an independent, and there is nothing worse than a person who thinks they know what they're doing and is stubborn about changing.

As I have indicated, my recruitment and on-boarding processes are very informal. If I like the look of an applicant, based on a combination of their CV and their specific pitch to me, I will invite them to drop by for a chat. If they make a good impression and we have a vacancy, I will invite them in for a trial few hours. They will be paid for their first full shift, but it is effectively a training or shadow shift when they are an extra member of staff, which makes it a relatively expensive process for me.

At the 'interview' – usually a cup of coffee in the Kaffe at a quiet time of day – I will have explained that we are too small a business to carry specialists, certainly out of the kitchen. This means we all have to be prepared to do everything – my favourite analogy is with the 'total football' developed by the great Dutch teams of the 1970s – from making coffee to clearing tables to operating the till – up to and including cleaning the premises from top to bottom at the end of each day. This requires flexibility and adaptability, and I hope it means the job is varied and interesting.

We don't have a long list of written instructions for new staffers to commit to memory, but we do have consistent ways of making coffee and presenting cups and plates which we run through on that first trial shift. Ideally, new recruits are sharp enough to pick these up first time. I expect staff to engage with each customer who enters the premises, but there is no script: each person should be free to bring their own personality to the job, and to behave in the way that comes naturally to them.

THE (UN)WRITTEN RULES
- greet each customer on arrival
- say goodbye to each customer as they leave, if possible
- don't chew gum
- clear each table when a cup/plate is empty, wipe down after each customer leaves
- on break, do not sit at one of the best tables or in a window, so a customer who arrives can't find a decent seat
- no smoking on the doorstep (see above)

We might not have a formal training programme, but we do have evening sessions every month or so after hours when we can practise specific skills, work towards consistency of approach, learn about new products, and have the sort of discussions that are simply not appropriate or possible in front of customers. These sessions are also good for team building, giving staff the chance to interact and get to know each other away from work time (unlike a restaurant, where prep starts hours before the first guests arrive, we tend to go straight into customer-facing work at opening time). I also make sure I pay staff the hourly rate for their attendance, which is only fair, but it also underscores the fact that these are work sessions, designed to improve the smooth running of the shops.

I also believe staff away-days, when we visit roasters or other businesses which are doing things particularly well, or even another city for a weekend, are extremely worthwhile. They might be expensive, but I see them as an investment in the business, and they are invariably followed by a leap in performance and engagement in the following days and weeks.

RECRUITMENT

When hiring staff for general roles at Darcy's Kaffe, I am not primarily interested in the experience candidates already have under their belt, so long as they can make a decent cup of coffee. Naturally, I welcome any new skills and good ideas that recruits can introduce to our business from their previous jobs, but these tend to be extras that I don't plan for except when hiring specialists.

The following is a rundown of what I am looking for.

Character attributes
Positive, upbeat, gregarious.
Not necessarily an extrovert, but the sort of person who likes to stay inside their own private bubble will not be suitable (there's a whole vast tech industry out there for them to work in).

Likes people.
We all like our friends, but good hospitality staff have positive feelings towards humanity in general. They are not wary of strangers; they are interested in all our guests, whatever their foibles, and strive to meet their demands and put them at ease.

Likes children and animals.
A surprising number of adults with children of all ages and dogs of every description visit coffee shops. All are welcome (except the badly behaved) and catered for (bowls of water outside for dogs in warm weather – which also encourages them to stay outside, which is usually for the best).

Liking children and animals is also a good litmus test of character. Nobody these days will admit, even perhaps to themselves, that they are uncomfortable with disability or racial and cultural difference, but in my experience if a candidate admits that they don't like babies or dogs, it might be a warning sign of deeper-seated prejudice.

Open mind, quick learner.
I find myself using the expression 'dialling in' probably too much. In the world of coffee it has a specific meaning, where it refers to calibrating the espresso machine and grinder to the correct levels for a particular brew

recipe. But I also use it with an older metaphorical meaning that harks back to pre-digital days, when listeners would tune their radio to certain frequencies in search of their favourite radio stations.

In terms of coffee shop staff, this means hiring somebody who will quickly adapt to the culture of Darcy's Kaffe – tune themselves in, as it were. In the best candidates and most successful hires, this will be a partly conscious, partly instinctive process of acculturation, involving listening, observation and imitation in order to fit in as seamlessly as possible.

Some cafés produce a booklet that is given to all new recruits, with a detailed rundown of tasks required and how to conduct themselves at all times. We don't, in part because I think this sends out a corporate-style message that can be over-interpreted so staff concentrate more on following the rules than on looking after customers.

I believe I make clear what is expected of staff both in conversation and through leading by example – with manager-level staff also showing the way. And by leaving the individual to find their own way to 'dial in' to our culture, they will do so while retaining their own personality – and may well expand our culture through their own unique contribution.

CREATE A CULTURE: MAKE THE EFFORT

Creating the right culture is absolutely key to lasting success, particularly as your business expands. To me, this culture boils down to one simple phrase: *make the effort*. It may sound simple, but it can be difficult to execute consistently, and it applies across the board. It is also tremendously powerful: if you make the effort to produce a decent cup of coffee, and if you have the necessary equipment, then I believe you can't fail. If you make the effort to interact on an individual basis with every single customer, they will notice and appreciate it. If you make the effort to keep the coffee shop spick and span, that effort will show and be rewarded. So this culture of *making the effort* should be a red thread that guides you through every aspect of planning and running your coffee shop.

If you have established this culture of making the effort and you recruit receptive staff, they will internalise the culture and the standards expected of them and will therefore behave in the correct way for their own reasons – and not simply because they are frightened of being ticked off by the boss.

I also believe that the individual culture you can offer as an independent owner-operator is quite different to anything the chains can manage – even the smaller, more specialist groups. Their managers simply won't care as much as you do. Even if you have the money to operate a full staff from the outset and you lack barista skills yourself, it's a good idea to find a way to work alongside your team rather than running the operation from a table out front or an office elsewhere. By doing so, you can lead by example and really set the tone for how the business should operate.

At Darcy's Kaffe, I set the culture by having specific standards I want to adhere to. I make no claim that it is necessarily 'better' than the culture somewhere else. It developed from the earliest days of the business, when I was operating alone. But as the business and the team grew, I made sure that I stayed on the bar, serving guests and making coffee, making sure that the new hires got to experience at first hand the culture of service I wanted.

It is also worth noting that the culture of a café is something that develops organically, whether you think about it or not. It can be a negative force: a survival culture of cutting corners, of getting away with minimum effort and engagement. This can take hold and may well strangle the business – so make sure you create a strong, positive culture.

THE ROLES

I have made it clear that, to begin with at least, every member of staff in the coffee shop has to be prepared to do a bit of everything, from preparing cups of coffee to plating up sandwiches to running the till. As the shop becomes busier and the staff larger, demarcations will tend to develop and specialists may well be hired. This has certainly been my experience with Darcy's Kaffes, where after almost five years I have senior baristas; a group of managers, each with specific areas of responsibility; chefs who only work in the kitchen; and a highly experienced baker who runs our bakery.

Much as I enjoy the actual process of making coffee (see box on 'The Flow' on page 131), when I work a shift in the Kaffe I tend to operate in a floating role like the shift managers, lending a hand where necessary while also working the front of house, greeting regulars and so on. I also believe that some sort of rotation is necessary between making coffee (we have two baristas on at busy times) and handling the till.

Between them, these two staff roles are key to customer satisfaction: the barista must ensure that every cup of coffee is pretty well perfect, while the person manning the till is the point of contact with each customer. Many coffee shops put inexperienced or even new members of staff to work on the till, on the basis that this is where they will be best placed to learn about the business and its quirks. Others – and I would count myself in this camp – see this as a mistake: if the person at the till is a bit lost and uncertain, that uncertainty is communicated directly to the customer. Doubts set in, orders are misunderstood or muddled, the orderly 'flow' that ensures nobody waits too long for their drink even during busy periods is interrupted.

In fact, the person at the till has to be simultaneously maître d' and quarterback: hosting each customer, sorting the takeaways from the sit-ins, explaining the menu, dealing with payments, spotting trouble before it has happened, firing off orders and instructions to barista colleagues and the kitchen. During busy times it can be absolutely exhausting; you're working on multiple fronts simultaneously, never truly able to concentrate on one. Speaking personally, I can happily lose myself in making coffees for six hours at a stretch, but I'm shattered after three hours at the till, in desperate need of somebody to take over from me.

As Darcy's Kaffe has expanded its offer, adding the bakery and a more substantial lunch menu, I have begun to receive job applications from some seriously impressive chefs. When baristas with impressive CVs approached me, I was flattered but perhaps not completely shocked: after all, we are working with some of the best roasteries in the world. But recently, a CV from an experienced chef in his late 20s landed in my inbox: he had worked at Noma, at L'Enclume in the English Lake District and at The Greenhouse in London, all of them among the best restaurants in the world and the most demanding of their staff. With a CV like this, during a period of well-documented chef shortages throughout Europe, he was clearly someone who could walk into a good job anywhere. Why did he want to work for us? After all, we don't even have a proper restaurant-standard kitchen, so what could be the attraction for him?

Like many applicants, the first thing he said in his message was that he had visited Darcy's Kaffe and liked the atmosphere. And it turns out that there are plenty of good reasons why apparently over-qualified chefs might want to join us. World-ranking fine dining restaurants are incredibly high-pressure places to work. They can take over your existence, depriving you of a normal social life and compromising your personal relationships. After half a dozen years, a chef may simply want to take a break for a while, step back and take stock of their career. They might want to be a bigger fish in a smaller pond (which Darcy's Kaffe most certainly is), away from the hierarchical world of fine dining, or they might be planning to start their own venture on a modest scale and reckon that there are things they can learn from me that they won't learn in a big-budget operation established decades ago.

Equally, they might simply want a normal job in pleasant company with evenings off in an attractive city for a season or two. Which is quite understandable and suits me fine. I make it quite clear that we are busy so it won't be an easy ride – but if they want to sample working life in a busy coffee shop and are willing to contribute a couple of good recipes, then they are more than welcome in our kitchen.

I'm also pretty sure that these top-class chefs are not applying for jobs in any other Copenhagen coffee shops. But they recognise our very real passion and ambition, even given the limited scope of our kitchen – no extraction fan! no fancy grill! no dehydrator! and so on. We want to create the most delicious sandwich or the finest pastry we possibly can; if possible, make it the best in Copenhagen. Our ingredients are sourced from world-class suppliers or niche local producers – people like the international greengrocer Natoora or the local Klippingegaard or Birkemosegaard, who also supply the likes of Noma and Kadeau.

MOTIVATING, INCENTIVISING AND RETAINING STAFF

One key challenge for cafés, especially smaller ones, is holding on to good staff when they've been with you for a while. First of all, it's hard to find good people and you've been lucky to have found them in the first place, or else you've invested good time and energy into training them up – either way, it hurts when you lose them, and staff turnover eats into your standards and resources, especially when it comes to key experienced people. Losing valued, long-serving team members doesn't just put a strain on your hiring and training hours, it can make it very hard to maintain the culture of the business.

Money

There are a number of ways to go about trying to retain staff but the most obvious one is *money*. This can't be avoided. You're probably paying the team a starting wage that's comparable to the market just to attract staff in the first place. But if you don't reward longer-serving staff – who, by default, start to take up more responsibility when it comes to shadowing/training of newer staff, whether they are counted as management or not – with increases to their wage, then you will fail to demonstrate that there is the possibility of progression as a reward for hard work and loyalty.

At Darcy's I promise to review salaries after the first four months for new hires and annually for other staff. While the salary does not always increase (it's hard in a small business to guarantee continual growth), I'm at least displaying the willingness to assess and reward performance, which normally leads to improved attitudes. A business where there is no such hope, no matter how small an enterprise, will struggle with retention. As the business gets busier and staff work harder, they should be rewarded to maintain their level of application.

Work Environment

Money isn't everything, however. It certainly helps, but most (good) people cannot be simply bought. If the work environment isn't up to scratch, if the work itself isn't engaging and exciting on some level, then you will struggle to retain good staff. Working as a barista or in other roles in the café usually means long days on your feet, lots of repetitive tasks using the same parts of the body (cue soreness), lots and lots of cleaning, early mornings and endless interactions with the public. It is not for everybody.

While this is what the job has to be, these hours can seem more or less manageable depending on staff morale and conditions. If you do your utmost to make the space as ergonomic as possible, to ensure that staff take adequate breaks where they don't need to deal with people (a break room would be the ideal), and to listen to staff comments regularly and act on them when possible, you can make sure the team can get through the day as comfortably as possible and that they *feel* heard – invaluable to keeping people on board and happy. We try our best to organise staff events every season, including a proper Christmas dinner somewhere nice and regular trips to suppliers and collaborators. These both inform and educate the team, as well as bringing them closer together and keeping them motivated. Other companies manage to do even more, such as our local friends Coffee Collective, where their big team all have access to physios as well as enjoying legendary staff parties.

Responsibility

Connected to but separate from pay is the question of giving staff additional responsibilities. The key here is that you're offering people the opportunity to feel they can achieve personal growth. This is important to attract ambitious applications in the first place. Then you need to provide staff with the tools and environment in which to learn. But once a barista has reached a certain level in your company, what can convince them to remain with you? The opportunity to try other things, to experience being a manager, or a roaster, or even a baker will offer potential paths to these skilled workers, who could easily take their knowledge to a competitor (and would have every right to do so). Of course, it may be the case that you simply don't have the capacity to give additional responsibility to an employee at a given time – we are of course talking about tiny businesses, not corporate structures with many divisions. But being open with staff about the company and its ambitions, and creating that culture of excellence we have talked about elsewhere, will go a long way to persuade people that they should stick with you for a bit longer.

LEGAL REQUIREMENTS AND RESOLVING ISSUES

Employment law varies from country to country, so you should make sure you are familiar with the rules that apply in your jurisdiction. I have a set contract which I exchange with each new member of staff, that lays out the responsibilities and requirements of both sides, including salary and hours.

People assume that you need a lawyer to draw up a contract, which makes it an expensive business. Wrong: a contract drawn up in handwriting, properly signed and dated by both parties, can be legally binding, but it can't override the laws of the land anyway so general employment law is still the key factor.

Given this situation, the contract I have drawn up is pretty much lifted from employment contracts I have signed myself in the past – contracts drawn up by lawyers in the first place, so why pay for the same work to be repeated?

Most often, the biggest problem you come up against as an employer is the misfit – somebody who turns out to be the wrong person for the role. We all make mistakes and I will admit that I have on occasion made a wrong call when recruiting staff. Usually it does not matter greatly: somebody assures me they are looking for a permanent role, they stay for a couple of weeks, then either something better comes up or they decide Darcy's Kaffe is not for them. No real harm done beyond the waste of my time and effort – although it is always a loss for me if somebody good leaves during their three-month probation period (when either side can pull out of the contract at a week's notice).

One particular case was quite tricky and took a few weeks to work out. I took on a barista from a coffee shop with a high reputation, who assured me she was passionate about the job and was ambitious to develop her skills. It turned out that she was passionate about developing her skills as a latte artist, which meant she was very slow in delivering each cup at busy times. She was also introverted and made no attempt to make alliances with colleagues or interact with customers. Worse still, she had a personality clash with one of my best managers, which meant they could not work together – and we are too small a team to be able to accommodate this situation. During her probation period, there were enough little incidents to convince us she was not a good fit, so eventually we sat down with her to explain that we had to terminate her contract.

FREELANCE WORKERS

Despite your best efforts to hire and retain a killer team, you may find yourself short-staffed at some point. This is not a great situation to be in for obvious reasons (everyone feels stretched and the stress of being down on team members is palpable) but it cannot always be avoided, sometimes due to situations beyond your control as we have seen in recent years with the pandemic. In some contexts, other contributing factors – such as Brexit in the UK – have put pressure on staffing for even the strongest businesses. In these tough times, there has been a rise in freelance labour, supported in some areas by specific platforms (Baristas on Tap, Need a Barista) designed to help out both businesses and workers by connecting them. Copenhagen is a long way from London or New York in scale, and luckily we haven't had to rely on filling gaps in our team with freelancers. I say luckily, because in my experience it can be tough to maintain standards and hospitality, not to mention team morale, in a business that relies heavily on freelancers.

What I would say is that it can be incredibly useful to have a network of friends and fellow coffee professionals who can help each other out in a tough spot. While I haven't asked a friend to help out behind the bar since the early days PD (pre-dishwasher), I have called up reinforcements for events and market stalls when we haven't been able to spare someone from the team. So by all means, have an auxiliary unit in the wings, but I wouldn't recommend repeatedly relying on people who are just turning up for the day.

DRESS CODES

Strangely enough, coffee shops have led the world in fashion trends since the turn of the century. The hipster coffee shop look – the beard, the plaid flannel shirt – became recognisable around the world and helped nudge even Michelin star restaurants towards a more relaxed and informal appearance. The trend went way beyond the wider hospitality industry: even investment bankers are increasingly dressing down – and not just on Fridays – as millennials rise to positions of power.

But it's clearly not just a free-for-all, and most people are still in thrall to dress codes whether they are aware of them or not – those Goldman Sachs bros know exactly which brand of chinos is appropriate to their station. So it is well worth thinking through how you and your staff present yourselves in your coffee shop.

There are two main factors to bear in mind: coffee shops are by definition places of informal relaxation, so an overly rigid dress code for staff feels wrong; but they are also places to eat and drink, so a visibly high standard of cleanliness is required. A third consideration may also come into play: how to differentiate staff from customers?

Our basic codes for dress and appearance at Darcy's Kaffe are based around common sense and not written down – anybody who has worked in the industry before should know the fundamentals:

- you and your clothes should be clean, with no holes or stains;
- hands and especially nails should be scrupulously clean and washed with soap and hot water several times a day;
- long hair should be tied back or otherwise restrained if it is likely to dangle in plates or cups;
- dangling or chunky jewellery, including rings, should be removed during the shift;
- smokers should wash their hands before a shift (and by the way, nipping out to have a fag on the back step during your break is an absolute no-no. I understand that people have the right to smoke, but they should head for the local park or take a long walk to do so, then wash their hands before interacting with customers again).

Beyond this, we want our staff to be themselves, and self-expression is very much part of it. As for what customers have the right to expect, I think even our most buttoned-up and conventional guests these days expect to see tattoos, piercings and radical hairstyles on hospitality staff – they may even be part of the show.

While uniforms are probably not appropriate in independent coffee shops – even corporate Starbucks relaxed their dress code a few years back in a bid to tap into the relaxed coffee vibe – at Darcy's Kaffe we have thought long and hard about wearing uniform aprons. Interestingly, we have come up with two different conclusions for the two sites we currently operate.

In Rantzausgade, staff wear a uniform blue apron, both for practical reasons and for identification. The coffee shop is a large space with a semi-open kitchen, so customers can struggle to work out who is working there and who is a fellow guest – an understandable problem that led to several embarrassing conversations before we introduced the apron. Most members of staff appreciate the advantages of wearing the apron – and every now and then, it saves what might be their favourite T-shirt from a ruinous coffee stain.

Frederiksberg is a much smaller space with the bar to your left as you enter the shop and no more than two people working at a time. It is pretty obvious who is staff, and wearing an apron would seem somehow over-emphatic and unnecessarily corporate in this context – so we don't bother.

If you do choose the apron route, it is worth remembering that it is a practical garment that will get much heavier use than, for instance, a jacket on rotation in your cupboard. It will be worn every day and possibly laundered two or three times a week, so it is worth investing in a design and material that can withstand repeated washing and even looks better with a bit of age.

THE FLOW – A STATE OF PURE BEING

The feeling of flow we all know, when we are so deeply immersed in something that we lose track of time and who we are, has a neurological explanation: In a state of flow, the activity in the frontal lobe is reduced, it is almost shut down – and it is in the frontal lobe that the ability for abstract thinking is situated, the planning for the future and the sense of self. Everything that makes us human, in other words, and that makes perfect sense: You lose yourself and sink into a state of pure being, like an animal – belonging to the world, not to yourself.

Karl Ove Knausgaard in the *New York Times*, summarising neuroscientist David Eagleman's book/PBS series *The Brain*

People are sometimes surprised when I tell them that what I enjoy most about my work is actually making coffee. It seems too stock a response – surely an over-simplification. How could making a cup of coffee be that good?

Well, I can assure you that there is nothing I enjoy more than a busy shift making dozens of cups of coffee, one after another. I may well be shattered at the end of it, but the time has whizzed by and I have spent the hours in the sweet spot of what athletes refer to as 'the zone' or musicians 'the groove'.

Indulge me while I quote the Hungarian-American positive psychologist Mihaly Csikszentmihalyi, who identified and described what he called 'flow', the optimal state of

> being completely involved in an activity for its own sake. The ego falls away. Time flies. Every action, movement, and thought follows inevitably from the previous one, like playing jazz. Your whole being is involved, and you're using your skills to the utmost.

Csikszentmihalyi saw this highly focused mental state as a more reliable source of pleasure and lasting satisfaction in life than the more obvious pursuits of money or the gratification of desire. It is also a state conducive to creativity and productivity. Anybody who watched the 2022 World Cup will recognise that, for all the riches that his skills have brought him, Lionel Messi gets the deepest pleasure simply from playing football at the sublime level that his talent and life-long training have made possible.

Importantly for 'flow', making a good cup of coffee offers the level of skill and challenge necessary to create the conditions for this happy state of heightened absorption. Sure, there is an element of repetition – as there is in hitting a tennis serve, trapping a football with your 'wrong' foot, or playing an A-flat major scale – but a competent barista is forever making micro-adjustments in the pursuit of consistency and perfection, or to tease out the flavours of beans from differing origins and levels of roast (just as a player like Roger Federer makes instinctive adjustments to cope with variations in wind, in atmospheric conditions or the tension of the tennis balls used in a particular tournament).

In this, 'flow' is quite different from the big decision-making process that is involved in outright creation – a process that can be very stop-start, two steps forwards and a yard back, at times frustrating, agonising, full of false steps and erasures. In flow, you're doing something challenging with the confidence that comes from having pretty well mastered the skills involved.

'Flow' might seem to be an internalised, almost meditative state that functions at the level of the lone individual, but as at least two of the examples above should suggest, it also applies at the level of the team: for Lionel Messi or jazz trumpeter Miles Davis to experience the zone at the highest level, they need teammates or bandmates to function around them in parallel flow (and even Roger Federer needs an opponent of a decent level to push him there). I recently filled in at a friend's coffee bar when they were short-staffed one morning and got real pleasure from slotting straight into the routine of their three-strong team, hardly exchanging a word as we worked in harmony together, each one of us aware of what the others were doing and responding accordingly.

So while I might be selfishly happy in my barista flow, I know that I can only really get there if there is somebody good on the till orchestrating orders and payments, if the waiting staff are clearing tables efficiently and the kitchen is running smoothly. If any of these break down, I (or whoever is on barista duty) will have to pause in our coffee making to help fix the problem. Our concentration will be broken, and that flow – the ability to knock out a succession of slightly different coffee drinks fluently and at speed – will grind frustratingly to a halt.

On an ideal day at a coffee shop, each individual member of staff will be in their own flow, but will also be part of a bigger and more powerful team flow throughout the day that leaves them satisfied at the end of their shift. They will also have been a more productive team, helping to create the happy, buzzy atmosphere that attracts customers and turns them into regulars.

Of course, this is an ideal that cannot always be achieved: it can be difficult finding a flow when you're working the till and dealing with a succession of customers with widely differing demands and expectations; meanwhile, some members of the team might be working with you not because they want to, but because they need the money (a perfectly respectable aim in itself, but not the best recipe for job satisfaction).

Whether or not this perfect state is attainable, I believe that anybody running a coffee shop should do all they can to create the conditions where this 'flow' can flourish. Baristas should have everything they need close to hand, with clean and well-serviced equipment and fresh cloths in the right place. Every member of staff should be properly trained in their role, so they know exactly what is expected of them and where everything is kept.

I don't really like the term 'discipline' because it implies both force and constraint, neither of which contribute to a hospitable atmosphere – so I see it in terms of staff slotting into a way of doing things that is as frictionless as possible.

10 DESIGNING SPACE AND ATMOSPHERE

The external and internal look; snap judgements; getting the layout right; colour; furniture, old and new; lighting; music.

There is little point in me attempting to set down the design for an ideal coffee shop – if such a thing exists. There are no set rules, no non-negotiables. Most people who open one have to work with the premises they find and can afford; they have no choice but to make do, adapt and improvise. Some might be fortunate enough to have the blank sheet of a newly built unit to work with, or a beautiful old building with instant charm – but even here the dimensions and basic shape will be beyond their control. So the best I can offer is advice on what to think about when you set about your design.

If you have a large budget and a long lead time, you can probably afford to hire a specialist architect or designer who will transform your site, shifting walls, installing state-of-the-art lighting and fully foldable picture windows complete with awnings, and commissioning craftsmen to make purpose-built furniture to a one-off look. The rest of us – and that includes me when I opened the first Darcy's Kaffe – have to find ways of turning unpromising and possibly awkward-shaped spaces, lacking clear access to daylight as well as proper plumbing, into somewhere that can attract and welcome customers.

I have to confess, though, that when I put myself in this category of do-it-yourself coffee shop start-ups, I am cheating more than a little. My partner, Scarlett Hessian, is a highly accomplished architect with plenty of experience in designing interiors, both domestic and commercial. She is ultimately responsible, and therefore credited, for the entire project and aesthetic: she took the lead on every design aspect, devoting long hours to trawling flea markets and websites for furniture, helping to shift said furniture and equipment – all while looking after her professional clients and teaching at Copenhagen Architecture School. Most, if not all, of the information and ideas in this chapter are hers – so I acknowledge my enormous advantage and thank Scarlett for allowing me to share so much of her hard-won knowledge in these pages.

In her professional work, Scarlett is by definition designing for clients who have a reasonable budget to play with, so the advice both aesthetic and practical she gave me was pitched at a rather different level to her usual brief. She learnt a lot about working with a minimal budget when we set up Darcy's Kaffe, and here she shares those learnings – the short cuts, the surprises and the potential pitfalls, some of which we avoided, others of which we have to put down to bitter if productive experience: after all, if we learn from our mistakes, they weren't in vain.

SCARLETT HESSIAN ON DARCY'S KAFFE

As an architect, I can honestly say that this 'commission' has been the most satisfying of my career. That might seem strange, given that it has been the most restricted in some ways – particularly when it comes to budget. Normally, a client and I can agree that something specific is required, and I will go out and design or buy it – taking cost into consid-eration, of course, but with a fair degree of latitude in many cases. With Darcy's Kaffe, certainly in its first two incarnations, there was no budget at all, so I could not simply have an idea and put it into action; instead, I had to approach the task from back to front, finding things that cost next to nothing then deciding whether they would work, perhaps with a lick of paint or a bit of modification. It also meant I had to be a lot more hands-on with this project, actually building and painting myself as opposed to tendering for the job and selecting suitable contractors.

There is a real satisfaction in working successfully within a tiny budget: it is an affirmation of your basic skills and vision that you didn't need to throw money at the project to achieve pleasing results. There is also the satisfaction of improvising, of bringing together simple and inexpensive ingredients in such a way that they really sing together.

There's also a lot to be said for having kind, generous, talented friends who believe in the project you are working towards. I can't really claim all the credit for Darcy's, as my best friend Sanderson Bell (Sandy), who has his own design practice, was my sparring partner, wingman, shoulder to cry on and 2 a.m. drinking buddy while building window seats and assembling an Ikea kitchen.

But I am really talking about something else entirely when I describe the Kaffes as my proudest achievements. Usually when I have completed a project, I assemble a folder of all the visual and design documentation, the before and after photographs which show how I have transformed a space, and file it in a cabinet. Then I walk away from the project, in all probability never to see it again.

But with Darcy's Kaffes, I have something quite different in the form of an ongoing relationship with the spaces. In the normal course of my work, I hand over a pristine interior to my client, who might, for all I know, ruin the effect with an ill-chosen painting or piece of furniture, neglect it in ways that do it harm, or sell it on to somebody who has quite other ideas of how to use it. With Darcy's Kaffes, I can witness my designs being put through their paces, being stress tested over weeks and months by the ebb and flow of staff and customers. It is fascinating to see how the patterns of usage I imagined when I was in the design phase play out in real life, and I can and often do sit at a corner table sipping coffee while I witness the design in action, in a way that might be positively creepy if I sat in the restaurant (or even private home) of a conventional client.

Of course, this also means that I can carry on tweaking the design as potential problems or improvements come to light. A coffee shop interior is not set in stone, but is a flexible space that needs to be able to react and change in tune with the demands made on it – the move away from takeaway to sit-down as the Covid pandemic receded, a larger bar to accommodate more of a display etc.

I have even found myself developing a real attachment to the Darcy's Kaffes: if I've been too busy to drop in for a couple of months, I find myself missing them and can't wait to get back to see what might have changed in my absence – the sort of intense feeling you normally only have for a beloved home.

GENERAL APPROACH

In earlier chapters I have encouraged prospective coffee shop owners to be open and to feel comfortable with seeking advice from people who are a few years down the line in the industry. When you get to the point of physically opening your own shop, I would go further still and encourage you to involve friends who are not necessarily in the industry – you will be amazed how enthusiastic most people will be, offering to help shift furniture, even paint your walls. After all, you're setting up a community asset – a sociable meeting place – not a purely commercial venture, a firm of solicitors or a funeral parlour, so your early customers will most probably be people you already know. And you may well be more interested in coffee, or in people, than in design – so pick the brains of your most stylish friends. You won't have to follow their advice, but it could help you generate ideas.

This approach extends to your new neighbours, including the people who run or work in the businesses nearby. You may find it awkward to introduce yourself to other coffee shop owners – your future rivals, after all – but everybody else will be people you hope will spread a good word about you, and they will most probably be delighted at the prospect that you'll bring new trade into the area. Ask their advice about local trade, busy times, potential problems with the council or whatever – they'll be flattered. And once you have actually opened, invite them to drop in for a coffee on the house, the perfect ice-breaker.

KERB APPEAL

The real-estate mantra 'location, location, location' contains a lot of truth. The exact location of your coffee shop will have an enormous bearing on the number of coffees you manage to sell. But it is also true that the better the location, the higher the rent – so a 'better' location does not always translate into a better business.

This means there's no need to despair if your tight budget means that you'll never be able to afford a prime spot for your dream coffee shop. Some of the most expensive premises are bang next door to railway stations, tourist traps or in ritzy shopping streets. Yes, you'd certainly be able to sell a lot of cups of coffee there, but most will be to ephemeral passing trade rather than to regulars, which means you might struggle to create the sort of atmosphere you aspire to. A high rent will also make it more difficult to record a profit. We will look more closely at this in Chapter 12, but a guideline is that your rent should never exceed 10 per cent of your sales turnover.

My first coffee shop was at the opposite extreme: a semi-basement site down a side street which hardly anybody used. This meant there was a lack of potential passing trade, from people dropping in en route to somewhere else – visitors I could hope to convert into regulars. It was also a site that suffered from a lack of daylight, with just one brief moment in the day when the sun would bounce off an apartment window and grace the front bench. So at the beginning the Kaffe was effectively 'by invitation only': people who knew me personally or who came across me via Instagram, plus any contacts they brought along.

It was all I could afford, so I made the most of it, with plenty of Ikea hacks – and it was quiet enough that I could run it on my own, so I did not need to shell out on salaries. In retrospect, it was probably a good place to learn about running a business, with sufficiently low overheads that I could just about make a living. But it is not a tactic I would necessarily recommend and there are risks attached: on the one hand, you may find yourself locked into a longish and inflexible rental agreement; on the other, if you move to better premises a few miles away, you risk losing the goodwill and regulars you have managed to build up. In my own case, I was extremely lucky; after I had been at my first address for about 12 months, I found a much better site within easy walking distance, which meant I could take my existing regulars with me when I moved.

As described in Chapter 5, the new Darcy's Kaffe, now my main venue, occupies a ground-floor corner in a residential area beside a busy street used by thousands of cyclists commuting to the city centre, a couple of kilometres away. This gives us two separate if overlapping sources of trade: people who live or work nearby, and people who cycle past twice a day on their way to work and home again. In fact, it is hard to exaggerate the many advantages of a good corner site. Not only is it automatically more visible and eye-catching than a simple shop front, it also has people passing along two different axes, and from the design point of view has two sets of windows, meaning more natural light. In my case, the smaller street to one side has only one-way traffic, but there is plenty of room for tables and chairs on the pavement – yet another benefit of the corner site, more than doubling our capacity in warmer months.

Before we moved in, the site was unproven despite its clear potential. It was very much on the fringe, sandwiched between a cool and thriving area with some other like-minded independent businesses and a major, quite unpleasant road. There had been nothing here before to draw a crowd, and the proximity of heavy car traffic and the lack of public seating meant that nobody lingered in the area.

So before making a commitment to the new site, I put my post-graduate training as an urbanist to good use – and the more I stood outside at various times of the day, counting the people who walked or cycled past, the more convinced I became that this was indeed a prime location for a coffee shop. There is nothing particularly scientific about this methodology and you don't need to have studied town planning to put it into action. Before taking on a prospective site, simply station yourself directly opposite at various times on different days of the week, in different kinds of weather, to gain a good understanding of the flow of people in the area.

One further attribute of the building drew me, and this was almost spooky: I had always fantasised about having a coffee shop painted dark blue outside – and sure enough, this building was painted a beautiful dark shade of blue. So it felt somehow inevitable, even preordained, that I would move here – and I wouldn't have to touch the outside beyond putting my name above the door.

Within a week or two of opening, it was immediately clear what a tremendous difference the location had made. Yes, the exterior and interior were more visually inviting and generally superior to those of my original basement, but the main reason for the extra custom was visibility: with so many people passing, it was inevitable that a proportion would drop in at least once to see what was on offer. Fortunately, many of them seemed to like what they found.

SNAP JUDGEMENTS

Contrary to the old saying, you can indeed judge a book by its cover – we all do so, every day, because there are so many instant judgements we need to make. This is particularly true of the retail and hospitality industries, which is why branding is a multimillion-dollar business.

The big national and multinational chains have an immediately recognisable brand identity that signals to passers-by exactly what they will find inside, and they strive for consistency in delivering the same product across thousands of outlets. Independents are playing a slightly trickier game. Our external 'look' – the image that strikes the eye of the passer-by in a split second, on which they will unconsciously make a snap judgement – has to convey a genre or type as well as project a measure of individuality. If the shop looks too glossy, serious coffee drinkers may suspect style will triumph over substance inside. Too scruffy and the inference is that the proprietor doesn't really care: so will the coffee be up to scratch? The look should suit the location too: what might appear funkily laid-back in a New Zealand surf town would almost certainly look slack on a metropolitan high street in the northern hemisphere. Luckily for us coffee shop proprietors, stripped-down minimalism is still very much in vogue, so we don't have to spend a vast fortune on internal or external looks – I for one will always take seriously a coffee shop that is subtly understated about what it offers.

Ultra-clean windows, which both catch the light and reveal enticing glimpses of what is inside, look smart and also show that you care. It is also worth noting here that you and your staff should make a habit of cleaning up properly before you shut up shop at the end of the day. Leaving messy tables overnight is a tell-tale sign of neglect that could cost you dear with any passer-by who puts their nose to the window: no, they won't come back tomorrow. Making sure you clear any debris left outside at the end of the day (cigarette butts, gum, napkins etc) will help your shop to look appealing and will keep neighbours happy too.

Clear signage is important, so passers-by know the basics of your trade: coffee to stay or go; snacks and pastries; larger plates if that is the case. An A-frame chalkboard on the pavement is a surprisingly effective tool with deep symbolic value, waylaying passers-by and drawing the eye to what you have that is special today – without annoying people in the way that restaurant touts do in tourist traps. Once or twice we have hung the 'closed' sign on the front door and started cleaning the tables while forgetting the chalkboard outside. Invariably, a customer will knock on the window or barge in to demand a hot drink. We ask, as politely as we can, why they took no notice of the sign on the door. 'But your board is out on the street!' they retort – seeing it is believing. So do have a chalkboard, take the trouble to keep it interesting – and remember to bring it in at closing time. Have a look at some chalkboard inspo from around the world if you're struggling for ideas.

Once you have sorted out the signage, there are a number of smaller details that all add to the external visual attraction of a coffee shop. Some plants outside, either planted or in pots that you can bring inside when you close, are another good indication that you care – in much the same way that a nice vase of fresh flowers inside is a relatively inexpensive way to add to your atmosphere. All of these outdoor design elements help to give an indication of the character and quality of the shop inside, so it's important to consider carefully how you want to portray yourself.

If you're really not sure how the front of your shop should look, my advice would be to go for a walk around some of the neighbourhoods you like the most and take photos of the shops you are drawn to. Then break them down: How have they been painted? Do they have a bell on the door that dings when you walk in? How have they placed the furniture or flower boxes out front? Is there a dog loop by the front door so you can safely leave your furry friend in plain sight while you go in? The things you may need to be inspired by are all around you – you just have to open your eyes to them and ask yourself why you like them. Then borrow these ideas. As Mark Twain wrote:

> There is no such thing as a new idea. It is impossible. We simply take a lot of old ideas and put them into a sort of mental kaleidoscope. We give them a turn and they make new and curious combinations. We keep on turning and making new combinations indefinitely; but they are the same old pieces of colored glass that have been in use through all the ages.

EXTERIOR CHECKLIST

If you're not blessed with the perfect location with gorgeous windows to draw people in, there are still design changes you can consider to attract passers-by and tempt them inside.

- Paint the facade so it looks fresh and clean. This is a good signal that there has been a change of use to a place.
- To test ideas for your facade, take a photo as square-on as you can manage. Open it in Photoshop or Paint and draw around the windows to test colours, and perhaps even experiment with a mural. Drop images of your furniture, plants and signage onto this to see if it all ties together nicely. This can also be a useful way to ask friends and neighbours what they think, to make them feel part of the process.
- Have clear signage above the door.
- Put out an A-board which lists what you're selling.

- For signage, white writing on a black background is far more visible from a distance than black on white. You have to think about somebody who is new to the area: a travelling tourist who spots a large COFFEE will know what you're serving from 200 metres away.
- If your local council will allow it, exterior wall hanging signs are great long-distance signals. There are plenty of helpful businesses online which can make these for you and are fairly priced. Try Etsy or your local typographer or printing company.
- Place trees in big pots flanking the doors.
- Have outdoor benches or furniture. Make sure the design of these is in keeping with your interior aesthetic, to carry a design thread through the whole place. If you can, add seat cushions and a basket of blankets to invite people even on cold days. This also softens the look of practical metal outdoor furniture. Adding layers to an exterior space is tempting to customers and easier for the person who might not be able to bring a pram in or make it down the stairs to sit inside.
- Where is the sun in different seasons? What times of day do you get the sweet spot of sunshine? Do you have enough depth on your pavement for café tables and chairs to sit opposite each other? Is there room for parents to park their buggy while they enjoy a coffee? Is there anywhere to lock a bicycle?
- If you have the luxury of outdoor space, consider varying sizes of groups. If you have somewhere good to sit, groups will come together or arrange to meet up there.

GETTING THE INTERNAL LAYOUT RIGHT

When it comes to planning the interior of the premises, try to strip it down to the bare bones and think of the space as a whole before worrying about the details. Your first and most important decision will be where to site the service area – the bar across which you interact with customers. Ideally, this should be fairly close to the entrance, so guests don't have to think about where to go on arrival and so you can clock them as they cross your threshold. It should also be relatively easy for takeaway customers to exit without spilling their drinks over guests sitting at tables.

Ideally, with the flow through the space, you want people to arrive, be greeted and have their order taken, then move on to a waiting space beyond the ordering area while their takeaway is prepared, so the person next in line can step forward to order.

If you have two points of access to the street, you should designate one for Entry and the other for Exit, to establish a one-way system so customers are not doubling back through the queue. If this is not possible, then the space you leave around your service point is crucial. You need to have two clear lanes of traffic so people don't cross paths. Customers aren't always at their most accommodating at 7 a.m., so if you can make this experience seamless for them, they'll come back.

The most important thing is to avoid creating a pinch-point. If this isn't possible with the space you have, then your team will have to be really active at communicating to customers where to go once they've ordered to make way for the next customer.

On the other side of the bar – your side – it is important to plan for a comfortable workflow for baristas, front-of-house and kitchen staff, with good communications and efficient use of the space available. Traditionally, there should be at least 90–100cm between the front and back bar of a classic galley-style kitchen. This is the usual designation for just one person working in the area, which isn't often the case in a busy shop, but you are unlikely to get a more generous workspace when there is a premium on squeezing as many covers as possible into an interior.

The precise layout of your workstation is also a key consideration. Ideally, you shouldn't steam milk right next to the coffee grinder as the moisture coming off the steam wand could harm your machine. You need to consider where cups with espresso in them should sit while they wait to be finished off with either steamed milk or water. Will this space be enough when there are multiple baristas working together and on a busy day? How about the final handover to the customer: does it work well? And do you need to place a lid/sugar/stirrer/sleeve/rubbish set-up there for guests to use?

As for the placement of your beautiful new toy, the coffee machine, you can choose to have it on show on the front bar, which means you always face the customer while making their cup of coffee. But more often than not, pre-existing plumbing will dictate its placement beside the rear or side wall, and you may find yourself with your back to the customer and with the workspace exposed – as we do at both locations.

For legal and hygiene reasons you need to have a hand sink to wash staff hands if you are serving food and drinks, so make sure you don't forget this. Also consider a pitcher rinser if you have the space and you expect to get busy. This saves a lot of time compared with using a standard tap to clean jugs post use.

Where is your *knock-box* (a waste bin designed to take used coffee grounds from the espresso machine) going to live so it's practical but not in the way? It can be built into the bar or be freestanding (for instance, the Rhinowares Thumpa tube).

Where will customers put their rubbish?

You can use your ceramics for coffee and serving plates as a decorative element on a shelf as well as placing them on the top of your coffee machine to stay warm. All of these small elements contribute as design features of your brand.

The placement of your menu is also very important. Make sure everything is clearly labelled, priced or described so customers can inform themselves if you are in a busy moment and don't have time to describe every new tasty coffee or dish of the day. Like most architects, Scarlett loves an 8-point font, or print size, but I find that customers struggle to read it so I would choose bigger type:

This is 8-point type, which can be difficult to read.

This is 12-point type, which is easier to read.

This is 14-point type, which is clearer still, but may take up too much space.

ARRANGING SPACE

Think about furniture placement and distances:

- If you are only serving pastries, you can afford to choose a smaller size café table to allow for more space or extra seating.
- You need to consider chair sizes. Lovely as it is to have comfortable up-holstered chairs, when these are pulled out and someone slouches in them, they eat into walking space. Limit them to areas with less foot traffic.
- If you don't want customers to linger too long, install hard, backless seating.

Make sure you identify where existing pipes, electricity and drainage are located at the outset. Once you have settled on a site for the service

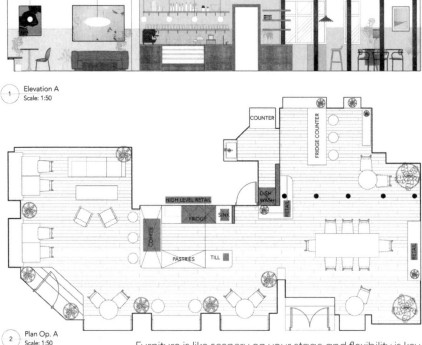

1 Elevation A
Scale: 1:50

2 Plan Op. A
Scale: 1:50

Furniture is like scenery on your stage and flexibility is key.

area, you need to think about where to place fixtures such as sinks that require plumbing: while almost everything can be modified later if you find the positioning does not work, plumbing is definitely worth getting right first time, and the more you have to move these services, the more expensive things will get. You also need to be clear about the functions of your service area and what is required in terms of storage, sink, dishwasher, refrigeration and so on – and of course coffee machines and grinders (see Chapter 4).

Plans, architectural drawings and computer-generated mock-ups can all be useful, but in my experience nothing beats marking out floor space with gaffer tape or flattened cardboard boxes to help you envision space (you may have seen Lars von Trier's film *Dogville*, in which Lauren Bacall, Nicole Kidman and other Hollywood A-listers were required to act their way through a taped-out set). If you have access to the empty premises before you move in, all the better – you can simply mark your 'service area' and walk your way around it. If not, map out the space in an empty car park or garden on a scale of 1:1. Then walk your way through while acting out various roles: takeaway or sit-in customer, server, barista and so on. You'll soon discover where the potential bottlenecks are if two people can't comfortably walk past each other, if a customer has to bisect the takeaway queue to reach a table or if access to the kitchen space is potentially blocked by the till.

Everything should be designed to make navigation as smooth as possible for the customer – both easy and tempting. There's no point in having a wonderful offering of cakes, nibbles and snacks if the person ordering coffee can't see them or – worse still – has to ask for them. Again, an easy-to-read menu should be displayed by the till. Some coffee shops go overboard with a handwritten scrawl offering too much information about provenance or roasting levels on their specials, which can be difficult for customers to take in. Keeping it simple has the added advantage that you can then have a good verbal exchange with any coffee aficionado who wants to know every last detail about your specials.

If you have a retail shelf – and I believe you should – place it where people queue so they can pick up a bag of coffee beans or whatever to take home with them. Supermarkets know this trick, and so do bookshops – think of the displays around their tills.

One design motif we developed at Darcy's Kaffe and repeated at the second site is to source vintage wood-and-glass shop cabinets to use as our front bars. Handmade in the Fifties and Sixties (but you can find pieces dating back to the 19th century) for ladies' and gents' outfitters, these are both attractive and practical while ticking boxes for upcycling and zero waste, and can be cheaper than commissioning a carpenter to create a contemporary equivalent. As well as showcasing the daily pastry selection, these give us loads of space to store resting kilo bags of coffee waiting to be used on the bar or sold retail, while still offering a nice visual on the customer side. When buying, note that you can haggle over prices for vintage furniture more easily than when ordering new or commissioning custom pieces.

We have established that the interior is a stage set that can and should be modified over time as the coffee shop develops its own identity. Takeaway might turn out to be a larger or a smaller proportion of your business than anticipated, or you might find yourself gravitating towards more serious meals, either of which would require tweaks in your layout and design. Furniture is like scenery on your stage that can be shifted around at will – even instantly if a party of eight turns up together for a sit-down coffee. Flexibility is the key.

THE BAR TOP

When we were creating our first permanent work surface areas for the bar and kitchen, we were alarmed at the potential expense given the cost of the materials (marble, zinc, stainless steel, solid wood, composites, concrete and more) and our lack of money. Panicking a little, we went to Ikea and found out that we could get a laminate approximation of real wood that didn't look too far off the real thing, for a fraction of the price. A couple of years in, we still have that surface at the bar, while in the kitchen we recently commissioned an affordable solid-wood replacement due to the higher intensity of use. The Ikea surface might not last for ever but it can be a good short/mid-term solution that will save you a lot of money.

FURNITURE

Think about whether you want to create a canteen or a cosy and inviting café. As you fit out the space, it is important not to be too obsessed by the number of covers you have, so don't be tempted to cram in as many tables and chairs as the floor can accommodate. People don't want to sit in a room dominated by furniture, so let everything breathe easy – it is amazing how quickly space gets eaten up. If you need your chairs to match, and it is significantly better value to buy them in bulk, work out how many is the maximum you can accommodate, buy them, but then keep a quarter or a third in storage until they are required.

Better still, buy as small a quantity of furniture as you can get away with and keep half your budget back. This way, you can slowly refresh the space over the months and years. Your regular customers will appreciate the stimulation of new additions and feel part of your evolution.

However chic those round wrought-iron tables beloved of French cafés may look, square tables are infinitely more practical and offer the flexibility you need. A table for two that still feels comfortable for the solo customer can swiftly become part of a table for four, six or eight.

When arranging your tables, bear in mind that people like sitting in corners when in public places – this is a primal human instinct that I was alerted to by the great Danish urban designer Jan Gehl. By sheer luck, the layout at Darcy's Kaffe comprises a series of window recesses, each one with a semi-enclosed window seat, which means that in effect our space offers eight corner seats instead of the usual four, where customers can sit in psychological comfort, surveying the scene in front of them while they sip and nibble.

When considering seating, remember that uniformity is not what you are always looking for in a coffee shop. At least three different seating heights are possible and all are welcome: standard chair, counter or bar stool, and sofa. Offering all three in combination can add interest and a sort of internal landscape to your space, enabling it to cater for different moods and combinations of people. As we have seen earlier (see Chapter 1), people frequent coffee shops on their own to a much greater extent than restaurants or bars, but they are also social spaces for couples, family groups, colleagues and friends to meet up.

I firmly believe that a mix of new and used furniture and fittings is ideal – and not just for financial reasons. Reclaimed and vintage pieces tend to have acquired a patina that adds to the *hygge* atmosphere of a coffee shop – the relaxed, informal vibe that customers gravitate towards. Yes, everybody likes to discover a 'new' coffee shop that serves the latest drinks and an original line-up of bakes, but at the same time they like the feel of something that has always been there, with the welcome of 'home'. 'New' can feel brash, stiff, shiny, perhaps a little cold and uncomfortable, somewhere you can't truly relax: using footwear as an analogy, trainers might be best when new, but an old-fashioned pair of handmade leather boots will be far more comfortable after being worn in and moulded around your feet for several months. If you do choose a more contemporary look, remember that you'll have to keep it spick and span – you won't be able to get away with the scuffs and chips that would be fine in a more rustic interior. As ever, you just need to think about that red thread of making an effort running through the design.

The main exception to this rule would be chairs – which, believe me, take one hell of a buffeting in a busy coffee shop. If you do buy used chairs, test each one very thoroughly to make sure it is robust. There are few things more embarrassing than a chair which collapses beneath the weight of a customer – embarrassing for both the customer, who will probably never darken your door again, and the owner, who may also end up with a hefty bill if anybody is injured. So whatever you do, don't cut corners with your chairs, and be prepared to buy new if necessary: they'll be a good investment.

A further word of warning on going down the second-hand route: if you have to kit out the entire coffee shop with what you can buy online for pennies in a couple of weeks, it will inevitably look cheap. The key to success when buying 'pre-loved' is to collect over time, so decide what you want and keep your eyes open on websites such as Facebook Marketplace and eBay, as well as flea markets, second-hand shops and the like. If you hear of any hospitality closures, you will often be able to pick up both furniture and equipment at knock-down prices. You will be amazed at the quality you can achieve by buying over a period of several months – and anything you end up not using can be kept back for later, if you have access to storage, or sold on in turn.

It is also worth testing any furniture before you buy it for the sound it makes when it is moved. Clangy metallic furniture whose every sound pierces the eardrums at the slightest movement is to be avoided at all costs.

STORAGE

One of the key challenges for smaller coffee shops is storage – both of what will be used today (coffee, teas, cups, napkins, milk, holders, bags etc) and what is being kept for a week or two (after all, you don't want to be organising daily deliveries from suppliers). In Chapter 6 we discussed the importance of resting roasted coffee beans to achieve the best-tasting drinks. Resting 30 kilos of coffee can put a major strain on your storage capacity if you don't have a basement or external storage.

One solution that can work very well in tight spaces is to build the storage into the furniture itself, so the benches that guests sit on are actually holding your stash of resting coffee and necessaries. This involves planning and designing from the outset, so make sure you consider your limitations on shelving and cupboard space before it's too late.

THE ENVELOPE

While I advocate sourcing select second-hand furniture with a patina from years of usage, it should always be contained within an immaculate 'envelope' – the walls, ceilings and floor which frame the space. A scruffy envelope projects a shabby atmosphere and shoddy, careless management: not the sort of place a guest will want to linger in (unless of course you are very consciously pursuing the ultra-boho peeling wallpaper look that has become increasingly popular in the last few years – in which case it works the other way round and the furniture needs to be immaculate, as at the Copenhagen design store Frama).

You may be lucky enough to inherit an attractive wooden floor, as I was in the second Darcy's Kaffe. This was not the case at the third, where we commissioned a micro-cement poured floor, which we then partially covered with rugs. Floors are very important acoustically, so it pays to avoid the type of hard surface that magnifies sound. If you have a new floor installed, make sure it is done to the highest standards and is absolutely flat: wobbly tables can be a real bugbear and staff in some coffee shops (cough) seem to spend half their time folding pieces of paper or cardboard to wedge under table legs.

COLOUR

When thinking about colour, you need to strike a balance between the conflicting requirements of projecting and reflecting light on one hand, and providing a feeling of warmth on the other. Note also that there is a very good reason why hospitals, schools and other institutional buildings have had two-tone walls since Victorian times, and probably earlier. The lower part of any internal wall, from just below shoulder height, will get far greater physical abuse in the form of bumps and spills than areas higher up – and dark paint can absorb mistreatment and hide marks much better than light. The same is true to an even greater extent for skirting boards, which take an enormous amount of punishment in a busy coffee shop. So while there may be very good reasons to paint walls in predominantly light colours, it is well worth considering a darker band closer to the floor.

However careful you are, and however well-run your coffee shop, you must be prepared to repaint your walls much more often than you would dream of doing at home. The good news is that a single coat can usually be completed overnight, which is ideal unless you are changing colour scheme and need several coats, which means you'll have to wait for a holiday closure. Another advantage of the two-tone approach is that you can repaint the lower, darker colour that gets all the punishment two or three times before needing to repaint the upper walls and ceiling.

When painting interior spaces, the colour you use where you serve food and coffee is important – you don't want to put people off their sandwich with a colour that makes them queasy, so be careful with lime greens, harsh yellows etc. It's a safe bet to opt for a more natural palette, which also helps to create warm, inviting spaces. For the most part, aim for colours with low saturation to avoid jarring effects.

In many ways, depth of colour is more important than colour per se. Colour should draw you in, not confront you. For example, if you love orange, don't pick 'easyJet' orange. Instead, find a warm, sumptuous orange that will add lovely, inviting layers to a space. Despite my love of blue (it's the café's official colour), it can actually be a tricky colour to get right. Steer clear of baby blue or turquoise as these risk transporting customers to the dreaded dentist or other medical centres – not the vibe you are after. If you want to use a lot of colour, it has to be done very well to be successful. Look up photos of the very pink Gallery at Sketch restaurant in London. The 'queen of colour', designer India Mahdavi, pulled this off and is highly sought-after for good reason. We have found it helps to think about how we would style a home – a domestic setting – and then put that into our commercial space. Our cafés have been described as like stylish Copenhagen living rooms – so we must be on the right track.

WALLS – ARTWORK

When the walls have been painted, the work doesn't end there. Artwork is an important decorative element that helps to reinforce or add highlights to your design. Working with local artists can develop your ties with the local community in two ways: it is a manifestation of your commitment to the locality, as well as offering a valuable outlet to local artists, who will be excited to have their work on show in a public space. Their pieces don't need to stay in place permanently – either they are sold to customers (creating a potential extra revenue stream, although you may choose to waive a fee in support of local artists) or different pieces are displayed for weeks at a time, keeping the café dynamic and fresh.

You might also want to use the artwork to bring attention to what you are serving. For example, your roaster may be able to provide pictures of the farm where your coffee is grown. The key thing with posters and photographs is to make sure you have them framed properly. A €5 (£4.35) postcard framed well with a mount can look perfect.

If you have large expanses of wall, it's often better to hang fewer, larger pieces of photography or art than multiple tiny pieces (see Studio Pepe for inspo on this). Scale is so important when it comes to decoration. While we've been lucky to find some local artists who agreed to loan us pieces, if you can't strike a similar deal and you don't have the money for art, then use wall paint to create change or character. Painting an offset square of contrasting paint on a wall can be decorative.

LIGHTING

This is a clean and pleasant café. It is well lighted. The light is very good and also, now, there are shadows of the leaves.

Ernest Hemingway,
A Clean, Well-Lighted Place (1933)

Lighting is vitally important to our experience of interior space and can have a dramatic effect on our mood. Many of us will have strong opinions on the subject, even if we don't recognise the fact; we struggle to explain what we want and what we like, however sure we are about our dislikes. In this section, I will try to offer some guidance on how to analyse your own views and then put them into action.

It helps to divide lighting into two broad categories: the purely functional, and the atmospheric or decorative. In a domestic setting, a single light fitting might have to serve both of these categories at once, but in a coffee shop you will probably need separate lighting systems to meet your requirements: brighter, more focused light for work surfaces, display areas and retail shelves – some of which may need artificial lighting even during daylight hours – and softer, more mood-enhancing lighting above the tables where customers sit.

In the two Darcy's Kaffes, we use ceiling spotlights for the functional lighting and stylish low lighting suspended over the tables. Denmark is world famous for its light fittings, so the expectations are high, and cultural norms also come into play: Danes like low lighting and often use candlelight at home; by contrast, while on holiday in Portugal I was surprised by the bright lights I encountered even in late-night bars.

Low lighting is also difficult to get right. We wanted to have a light hovering above each table, bathing it in an attractive glow, but we also wanted the lighting to look good from the street outside on dark winter afternoons – so where should we centre the light fittings? And what happens if you move the tables around to accommodate different sized groups? Inevitably we made mistakes, and every now and then somebody knocks their head against a low light fitting...

It is also worth familiarising yourself with the often confusing measurements of wattage, lumens and Kelvin. Power or strength tends to speak for itself, which leaves Kelvin as the measurement worth getting your head around. Broadly speaking, it describes the colour temperature of a bulb, ascending from 2200K, usually described as candlelight, through 'warm white' at 2700K, 'soft white' at 3000K, 'neutral white' at 3500K and 'bright white' at 4000K and above. For ambient warm light, 2700K tends to be the sweet spot, although halogen bulbs will push up to 3000K. Above 3500K, the light takes on the bluish tinge familiar from fluorescent lighting in hospitals; it may be useful for tasks, but is unpleasantly harsh for anybody trying to relax, so its use should be confined and angled away from customers.

One exercise you can do to help understand these different light levels and the effect they have is to walk down residential streets after dark and look into apartments (don't linger too long though!). By comparing different light sources almost as a cross-section, you quickly get a sense of the warmer end of the spectrum and colder, harsher lighting at the other end. Try to think about what your guests will respond to, and what feeling you want to convey.

Dimmer switches can be useful to add a degree of flexibility and control. Your needs may vary at different times of the year depending on your site's orientation to the sun, while the appropriate brightness level changes during the working day: early in the morning, customers are using their coffee and possibly breakfast to gear themselves up for the day ahead, and a little later they might be working over a cup of coffee. By mid-afternoon, though, people are looking for a mellower mood, and if you are open into the evening, perhaps for an event serving alcohol, the lighting should be toned right down.

You might also have your own tastes and quirks. I really don't like to see light bulbs at all – not just the naked bulbs which were a design feature of the extreme industrial look a few years ago, but bulbs protruding from the bottom of shades. It is generally worth indulging your own tastes in cases like this, unless they are too unreasonable or extreme – after all, you're going to spend countless hours in this space, and you'll only irritate yourself if you allow offences to stay.

Scarlett hates to see electric cords running along floors, walls or tables, which means we don't have many floor or table lamps in Darcy's Kaffes. This policy is fine and it does have its advantages: nobody ever trips up over a trailing cord or tugs over a lamp, and we never encounter the problems involved in moving a table with a lamp on it to a new spot that the cord can't reach.

But there are some attractive, brilliantly designed lamps out there, and the important thing to remember if you have multiple types of lights is to keep their design aesthetic on the same thread. For the main Darcy's Kaffe, Scarlett made the strict decision that all the lights, decorative or primary, had to be white. I didn't understand why until we had finished the space. We had found them over several months one by one, occasionally in pairs and if we were lucky in groups of three – but because they are all in a simple milk white, it looks like they were all purchased with much consideration and at the same time.

As for the problem of wires, there are ways of minimising the amount of visible wiring, especially if you have thought the problem through from the beginning and discussed it with your electrician before opening (as I have said before, wiring is one of the jobs you should not attempt to do yourself). Cables can be hidden away underneath or behind skirting boards or shelves, and sockets can be placed strategically close to the planned site of each lamp. It is also easy to upgrade boring black or white plastic-coated wiring with funkily coloured or woven cables that chime with your overall decorative scheme.

There are now some stylish wireless lights available at decent prices, which can be charged overnight. These offer flexible lighting in areas such as the bar or shelves where it would be tricky to have a cable trailing to a socket.

If you do have handily placed electricity sockets dotted around the interior, beware the customer who will brazenly unplug whatever you have in place in order to charge their laptop. Even without wired lamps, a coffee shop needs some sockets to power the vacuum cleaner and so on and I have known owners who go to great lengths to hide their sockets away in places that customers will never find, installing hidden doors or flaps in the skirting.

QUICK TIPS

- Choose your colour palette at the beginning. You can refer back to this whenever you find something you like, to see whether it will work.
- Less is more!
- Don't try to have more than one or two design themes running through your place or it will seem confused.
- Matchy-matchy doesn't have to be the case. Contrasting colours against timber furniture can be a nice touch.
- Water your plants! There's nothing worse than dead, dusty, crispy weeds.
- Have a consistent design thread through your coffee cups, plates and cutlery. Investing in high quality will show you care about what you're serving. A solid, heavy plate of food served with weighted cutlery can make a dish feel much more luxurious than a lightweight fork and a cheap china plate.
- Invest in lighting. It's the easiest way to upgrade your space.
- Use darker tones on upholstery – light materials show the dirt.
- Create zones with rugs, in durable materials such as jute, with natural colours or patterns to hide the dirt.
- Ikea carcasses are great for bars and kitchens and can be upgraded with stylish cupboard fronts. Ditto with work surfaces when on a budget.
- If money is tight, aim to create a timeless space that you don't have to change or update – a space that will get better with time.
- Don't over-invest in your interior until you feel confident you can keep the doors open. You can always renovate or upgrade as you gain stability.

DISPLAY DETAILS
Food

If you don't have the finances for a beautiful frameless glass fridge you can be creative with cake stands and plinths. We have always been inspired by the style and look of Ottolenghi shops – their feasts of food displayed in beautiful serving bowls stacked and layered over one another are hard to resist. You can find vintage cake stands and plinths for display online, which will help your kitchen's offering to stand out.

Retail

Your retail shelves must look intentional and not like overstock sitting there collecting dust. Make the effort to mix up stock and add seasonal items to keep people's attention. There's nothing less appealing than picking up a dusty item that's been sitting there for months.

Again, be inspired by shops you admire; borrow their ideas and make them your own.

Kitchen/bakery

If you have an open kitchen or bakery, or they are visible through a window, you absolutely must keep them clean, tidy and professional. High-quality produce can double as styling material – fresh vegetables or proofing dough placed artfully in full view showcase what you're producing. Stacks of dirty plates on show will have the reverse effect.

MAINTENANCE

You've done the difficult part and made a beautiful space that people love. Don't let yourself down by thinking the hard work is over and leaving the space to slide gradually into scruffiness. This is a commercial space that (hopefully) accommodates a steady crowd of guests, so chips, scuffs and coffee spills are inevitable (although you might find yourself wondering how that coffee stain got on the ceiling…).

Watching these small things and tackling them before they sit for too long is essential to keeping your space attractive and showing continual care. This will involve a regular programme of retouching and repainting the walls and maintaining the floor. Wooden floorboards will have to be sanded down and oiled every couple of years. This kind of attention is also applicable to cups, plates and glasses. Make sure you look after them well and take any with chips and cracks out of circulation – they are one of the first things a customer will notice. The more slick and clean your aesthetic, the higher will be the demands on maintenance – but don't use a rustic or shabby-chic look as an excuse to neglect the basics.

Health & Safety

Hygiene as well as health and safety are key elements to get right from the outset. Making sure you operate in a physical space that is safe for both staff and customers is essential, as you have a duty of care for those who pass through your doors to either drink or serve your coffee. It is also the case that properly cleaned and maintained equipment results in better-tasting coffee, so there is a real advantage to doing these things by the book.

Making sure that you operate in a clean and safe manner will also fill both staff and customers with confidence. All too frequently, as a customer in various hospitality venues, I have had the experience ruined by getting a glimpse of failings on the other side of the bar. I certainly hope none of my guests feel this way.

If you do slip up with the health and safety paperwork, which can be more onerous in some parts of the world than others – and I for one have been guilty of this – you can become a target for the inspectors, who will treat you with a greater level of scrutiny than might have been the case had you stayed on their good side.

RESOURCES
The following websites can be useful sources for inspiration:
Instagram
Pinterest
Houzz

To find second-hand furniture or equipment try the following websites:
eBay
Facebook Marketplace
Local classifieds such as DBA (Denmark), Gumtree (UK) and Craigslist (USA)
Vinterior
Pamono

MUSIC AND ATMOSPHERE
We can't talk about designing an interior without mentioning a crucial factor in the creation of a strong sense of place – music, combined with the acoustics of the space, is a powerful if mostly subliminal atmospheric tool. There is no need to install a costly state-of-the-art sound system unless

music is part of your theme (such as one of my favourites, Spiritland in London), but far too often I have been in apparently high-end coffee shops whose expensive fit-out has been undermined by tinny-sounding music from what sounds like a small old-fashioned transistor radio.

While achieving good acoustics can be a challenge, you can help yourself with the choice of materials and how you position speakers within the space. Think about adding soft furnishings such as seat cushions and upholstered furniture, and if you have a lot of hard tiles on the floor you could consider adding rugs, which can help mute sound as well as create zones. Speakers should be placed in corners directed into the room and ideally off the ground, allowing a clean distribution of sound through the space. As far as possible, try to work with multiple speakers in stereo to balance out the sound. If you only have one speaker source, your music is likely to be too loud close by and too soft at the far reaches of your interior.

Consider the different layers of sound in your space. Music can offer a background blanket that might help offset other less pleasant sounds such as the whirr of the grinder or the noise from a blender or mixer in the kitchen. The actual music you play is very much a matter of your personal taste, the demographics of your clientele and the atmosphere you are trying to create in your café. As ever, there are no set rules, but I can pass on a few tips based on my experience as in-house DJ (in my head) for more than four years at Darcy's Kaffe.

With my music selections, usually played from Spotify, I try to consid-er the average customer as well as being true to what I see as good music – which means playing what I am listening to at the time, but not the extremities of my taste. I think about what people are doing when they come into the café and spend time with us. They are not going to the gym or a nightclub and it might very well be their first interaction of the day. They might be coming in to work or to read a book, or they may be coming in to have a lively brunch with mates. I've been to many cafés where the music is so loud that you can barely hear your companion talk, and I've been to others where the music is so soft that you feel afraid to talk about anything remotely private because everyone can listen in. I try to strike a balance between the two with both the volume and the tune selections, aiming for something that can help lift the mood without making it difficult for people to concentrate or talk.

One additional important point to make is that the music is not just for the customers. Baristas and other staff might well be spending eight hours on the premises, so they need music to help them along – to stay energised and keep their spirits up in an atmosphere of good vibes enveloping both staff and guests. I always feel sorry for staff in shops over Christmas – who are subjected to a narrow 20-minute tape of seasonal classics, repeated on a loop through the day – so keep things varied, for your own sake and that of your team.

I am not personally in favour of prescribed playlists from the management or owner. Instead, I think it's much better to chat about the general aim for the music and then put your trust in your staff to carry out the DJ role in your absence. What can be really useful, though, is to create some collaborative playlists with your team that are saved on whichever platform you use; this will make it easy to find music that works, because nobody has time to mess around making selections when they're busy.

It's also important to think about different playlists for particular times of the day. We usually ease into the early part of the morning (from 7.30 to 9 a.m.) with something quite relaxing, such as Air's *Moon Safari* or Matthew Halsall's calming spiritual jazz albums. As things start to pick up and we feel like we need music with a bit of bounce, we'll switch gears to something like Cymande or Shuggie Otis. The rest of the day's mood depends on various factors such as the weather and day of the week. We might well switch to play some hip hop if we want another change of vibe – classic Nineties rap rather than gangsta rap or grime.

Public Lending Rights For Music

One of the things that caught me by surprise when setting up the second site at Rantzausgade was getting a visit from the Musicians Union of Denmark and subsequently a bill for the right to play music in a public place. I had probably flown under their radar in the less conspicuous basement space and I had actually had no idea about this fee – although it completely makes sense that some revenue should get back to the artists who help create a vibe in your business, rather than to Spotify. My brother Tom Millar is a professional jazz musician, so I'm in full sympathy with the union's demands.

Nevertheless, the fee was not insubstantial, especially at the outset of the move with so many other hidden costs to consider – so it is well worth doing some research about the local rules in your area to avoid getting a nasty shock. Music can indeed play a crucial role in creating atmosphere in your café but it might not really be necessary in some situations, such as takeaway operations, outdoor sites or cavernous spaces with lots of people creating noise.

11 MARKETING AND SOCIAL MEDIA

Building a social media profile; the power of Instagram; all channels in sync; branding your takeaway cup; the tuk tuk; retail options.

You take care to ensure that every cup of coffee is as close as possible to perfection, that every nibble you serve is fresh and tasty, that customers are properly looked after, entertained and given the promptest attention. You hope that they will come back again, and more than that, you hope they will mention you to their friends and that word of mouth – traditionally the best form of advertising – will work in your favour.

But there is still much more you can do to raise awareness of your business, to drum up custom, to spread the word that you are open – and this chapter will outline some of the most effective means I have encountered through a combination of research, luck and trial and error.

Traditionally, a new business might have advertised in a local paper, and these days many bigger businesses with more substantial finances behind them will invest in a marketing campaign. But, having opened Darcy's Kaffe on a shoestring budget and with the very lowest of expectations, this was not an option for me. Having launched successfully and found a growing niche in the market without spending a single Danish krone on promotion, it has never seemed necessary to invest cash in marketing.

If my working time is converted into money, however, I have invested a considerable amount in the business, by spending somewhere between 30 minutes and an hour every day on social media. This may seem a lot, and it is – but I believe it is time well spent and that repays the investment many times over.

I am not by any means a social media fan or a techie. I have never really used Facebook, and while I have a personal Instagram account, I only use it once a year – to post on my girlfriend's birthday. So it is not the case that I am a social media fan and it is my hobby. But I recognise that it is an enormously powerful tool if used judiciously – a direct and instant means of communication to my very specific target audience, with the potential to expand that audience in relatively quick time.

I also believe that any business in my field that ignores social media, or gives it insufficient care and attention, does so at its peril. Every day I see posts from companies – usually bigger than mine, probably run by a slightly older generation – who view social media as an irritating additional burden that has to be endured, so they farm it out to an office junior (the so-called 'digital native who understands that sort of thing') or an external marketing company (who might also give the task to a trainee). The result is often a misspelt message full of exclamation marks which entirely misses the point, because the writer does not properly understand the business in question.

So what does social-media marketing amount to in practice?

First, you need to think carefully about what will raise awareness of your business and promote it. Traditional advertising, whether it is in old media (newspapers, radio, television) or on the internet, works with massive numbers and is very scattergun, which makes it extremely expensive and only really viable to sell a product or service that is at the very least widely available – a soft drink, a breakfast cereal, a fast-food brand. There is very little point telling a million randomly chosen people about a small coffee shop in Copenhagen because the vast majority won't realistically visit it, even if they were minded to.

Ten years ago, having a good website was thought to be necessary for any modern business – and plenty of website designers made good money building them. All too often, the business owner felt no need to pay somebody to keep the website up to date, but was too busy or simply unable to do so themselves – resulting in a website that dated quickly and may even suggest the business has ceased trading. And there's nothing worse for a customer than seeing something you like featured on the menu of a website, turning up at the café or restaurant and ordering it, only to be told the said item is no longer available.

Many small businesses today don't bother with a website at all and simply use a company Facebook page to list the basic information of opening hours, address, phone number and email address for bookings. For Darcy's Kaffe, I've adopted a halfway house, building a website that is really no more than a landing page with basic information, so it does not require regular updates or invite any interaction. Nothing could be easier than putting together a front page with a bit of information 'about us', your address and instructions on the closest public transport or parking, plus a gallery of decent photographs to show you in the best light. If you want to go further, there are plenty of apps which will automatically use your social media feeds to update your website – although this is not something I do.

Instead, from the very earliest days of my business, when Darcy's Kaffe was no more than an idea and an occasional pop-up rather than a physical space, I put my whole communications focus on social media. I already had a pretty good idea of what I was aiming for through my own following of the businesses I was interested in and wanted to emulate – the best coffee shops and roasteries, some individual baristas, but also knowledgeable bloggers, travel writers, and anybody who seemed to have mastered the art of communicating via social media. These include but aren't limited to Friedhats roastery and coffee shop in Amsterdam, Oi Polloi menswear shop in Manchester, Siop Shop, a bonkers doughnut and coffee shop in Manchester, and recently Batch Baby coffee shop in London.

From the beginning, I was ordering coffee from the best local roasters I could and I would tag them in my posts. They would automatically receive an alert that I had tagged them, and in return they would send out a post saying that Darcy's Kaffe would be serving their coffee at such-and-such an event – advertising their own product, but more importantly, from my point of view, alerting their tens of thousands of followers to my existence. I gained by simple association: by being publicly identified as a purveyor of this particular top-class coffee, I had staked my claim as a serious (if tiny) player in the world of coffee. What's more, some of that famous roastery's followers would also follow me, particularly if they lived in Copenhagen or met me at an event where I was making coffee.

And this is essentially what I have done again and again, until now, almost five years later, I have my own 12,000 followers. And note, this isn't just a faceless crowd of people out there who may have heard of me vaguely in a coffee context, they are individuals who are specifically interested in coffee and who have made the positive choice to follow me. Many of them know my face and most would feel confident that, by following me, they have earned the right to introduce themselves to me when they drop in to Darcy's Kaffes – and I am certainly very happy when they do so. In short, this is a large but very precisely targeted group to aim all my marketing at and an extraordinary resource for my business.

To start with I also added hashtags to my posts, with the aim of reaching more people. But while this can certainly boost the number of users who find you in a search, they are not necessarily the highly motivated followers who come on board naturally or organically, so I gave up going down this route. For me, it is far better to know that all our followers have been introduced, as it were, rather than discovering us by chance.

Given that we now have so many followers, it is well worth me spending time on my communications with them. My aim is to use Instagram's 'post' once or twice a week, bearing in mind that each post is permanent, in that it remains on my feed indefinitely unless I make a special effort to delete it. So for this I will choose a better or stronger image – one that is a good reflection of the business, whether it is a scene or a close-up of latte art or a plate of food.

On top of that, every day I will post a number of 'stories' which last for 24 hours and is best for newsy updates on Darcy's Kaffe: a new item on the menu, the weekend's specials or a fresh retail line. This is not a hard sell, but a gentle invitation designed to give the customer an added reason to visit us, to generate a little excitement and the feeling that there is always something new to be tried that will justify dropping by. (There is the added possibility that if someone tags you as a story, you can re-use it, although I tend only to do this at the end of the day, to avoid muddling my main message of the morning.)

Clearly, given that we are a daytime business, the best time for my latest post or story to land in my followers' mobiles is soon after 8 a.m., when they might be checking through incoming mail and social media before launching into their day. Any later and my message risks getting squeezed out, skimmed over and perhaps even deleted before it impinges on their consciousness. One of the great things about this type of social media marketing is the very quick feedback: you can tell when a story hits home partly through the 'likes' pinged back, but also through word of mouth when a customer comes in and responds to the story – and through the till: I might run a story on an unusual coffee from a special roaster that has just gone on sale and assume that nobody cares very much because it generates no online traction. But when a succession of people drop in to buy a bag of those beans over the next few days, I know where the idea was planted.

It is well worth giving some thought to creating a consistent tone and aesthetic approach that you will use on Instagram to project your brand – without being overly commercial or corporate about it. I try not to agonise too much about the images and words, especially with stories, given that they don't last. But I find it best to draft the post or story the day before I send it out, then to edit and perhaps tweak it just before sending – a process that eliminates the worst mistakes that your fingers inevitably make. And – as I mentioned in the discussion of handling customer complaints in Chapter 8 – it is very dangerous indeed to post anything in the public sphere when you are tired, angry or disinhibited after a couple of alcoholic drinks.

If putting together an Instagram feed every day seems like a grind for somebody who would prefer to be making coffee (apologies for the dreadful pun!), you could put together a whole series in one slightly longer afternoon session in which you script out and photograph a whole run of new menu items for release one by one. This method can also be used to cover weekends or even whole weeks when you are away on holiday but still need to have an active social media feed.

I use Instagram for my business because it is what works for me as a customer and what is currently the default social media channel in the coffee industry. That might well change in the future, so it is important to keep your finger on the pulse of the industry and – if you'll excuse the switch of metaphors – to know which way the wind is blowing. It will be interesting, for example, to see if and how TikTok develops as a marketing tool. If you like the medium, give it a try and see if it brings you any trade.

I mentioned a few paragraphs back that one of the benefits of Instagram is that ability to re-use other people's content if they tag you. This potentially opens the door to one of the new worlds created by the growth of social media – the world of the influencer. Naturally, I have no objection to Darcy's Kaffe being recommended by bloggers and influencers, whether or not they ultimately send any trade my way. But when a self-appointed influencer requests a free meal in return for promoting us, I invariably turn them down politely – not so much out of any ideological scruples, but mainly because I doubt their effectiveness. As a customer, I know whose recommendations I trust and they are all bloggers who I know pay for their own food and drink.

I am always happy to cooperate with traditional local media, though, by giving interviews and providing photographs on request. And there are some freebies I'll happily provide in the right circumstances: so if a local charity approaches me for a donation, I'm always happy to provide a prize in the form of vouchers for coffee or a meal. I want the business to feel part of the local community, and I want the local community to feel that Darcy's Kaffe is theirs, so contributing in this way is a small price to pay for admission (as well as being better than simply handing over some cash).

A further benefit of social media is as a staffing tool. Yet another area where I have saved money is in recruitment: I have never used paid advertising or an agency to find new staff. Instead, likely candidates tend to have found me via social media and concluded from what they can see on my feed that Darcy's Kaffe is somewhere they would like to work, so they contact me directly. This very process ensures that there is some degree of cultural fit between us, whereas I know that if I relied on professional recruiters and general advertising, I would have to sift through hundreds of applicants whose idea of a cup of coffee is better suited to bigger, mass-market chains.

TRIANGULATION

One thing that is important to highlight is making sure your *different channels are all in sync* with the overall message of the business. You want to give an accurate representation of the space and vibe of the shop because obviously you're super-proud of it and you want everyone to know about it. But you also need to make sure people know what to expect, so don't create silly expectations that have to be met to avoid disappointment.

Instagram's free professional account will also give me useful updates on the previous 30 days: for instance, that I have 12,200 followers and have reached 14,400 separate accounts, including 5,300 non-followers.

Every now and again, I'll check Google Maps, Facebook, and perhaps do a quick search on Google, just to make sure everything is as it should be. I recently got a call on my personal phone number from someone asking if we were closed on a Monday (of course not – we open every day!). I then realised that we were listed on Apple Maps, complete with my mobile phone number and some incorrect information. I never even considered this as I deleted the app from my phone a *loooong* time ago, but now I have corrected the listing, making sure there are some nice photos uploaded there for any Apple Map users. (This sort of mix-up can happen to anybody: a fine dining restaurant near Liverpool was effectively declared closed by Google for six months in late 2022. Luckily the chef has a loyal following who knew better...)

So far, Instagram has been my main channel, but as I write, TikTok appears to be gathering momentum. I will keep a close eye on developments in social media, and change my focus if and when the time seems right.

THE TAKEAWAY CUP

When I wrote a few pages ago that I had invested no money at all in marketing, that did not tell the whole story. Very early on, it struck me that if I was going to buy disposable cups for takeaway, it made sense to spend a little more to put some branding on those cups. After all, every takeaway cup that leaves your shop is a potential mobile advertisement so to send your precious coffee out in an unmarked cup is very much a wasted opportunity.

Our first (and cheapest) method was to apply a stamp to plain takeaway cups, but this did not look great and was time-consuming. So as soon as we had the graphic of a person drinking a cup that we wanted to establish as part of our brand, we commissioned some takeaway cups in the distinctive blue of Darcy's Kaffe emblazoned with the design.

Ideally, the cup should be of a decent quality and clearly marked as compostable – both for genuine environmental reasons and to avoid offending our many customers with strong green sentiments.

It should be possible to find a supplier who will print disposable cups to your design on the internet. Failing that, find a disposable cup in your area that you like and look underneath – the company that made it will probably display their name somewhere. If storage is not a problem for you, try to order as many as you can because you will get a much better deal if you place a bulk order. Don't order until you have seen a prototype and approved it: seeing a design from your specifications dummied up on screen is not adequate and you don't want to be landed with a job lot of cups that are an embarrassment to your business.

THE TUK TUK

There are plenty of other things you can do to make your business visible and raise awareness of your presence, and in the case of Darcy's Kaffe some of them go back to the very origins of the business. I still set up a mobile stand at as many public and private events as possible, targeting any large gatherings of people, ranging from street and music festivals to art fairs and fashion weeks.

These can be very lucrative in themselves but are also a brilliant way of connecting with a new audience who happen not to live or work close to the two Darcy's Kaffes, or who simply haven't discovered us before. People attending these events are often in just the right mood to 'discover' you: they are in entertainment mode, looking for new things to see and do, hanging out socially with groups of friends or colleagues, often with a bit of time on their hands. So, unless there is a big queue waiting to be served, they will often ask questions and engage with us, taking down details of our shops for future visits. I tend to man the stand myself as much as possible; it is hard work, but makes an interesting change of scene from the usual four walls – which, however much I love them, can become routine.

To make outside catering easier to provide and more eye-catching, I invested in a second-hand tuk tuk that I found on Facebook Marketplace – a small Italian-made motorised tricycle, customised with a coffee machine mounted on the back and all the plumbing and power required to be completely mobile. I had it repainted in our livery blue and hand drawn by good friend and artist Carmen Lew. This is not a high-performance vehicle – it can barely make it up a hill, which is not usually a problem in a city as flat as Copenhagen, although I once had a hair-raising trip driving 10 kilometres north to a private party in the countryside at night in a snowstorm – but with a few upgrades to the coffee machinery (grinder and PUQpress – see Chapter 6) it is able to make unbelievably good coffee, pretty much anywhere! It is, after all, an ambassador for the brand so we put just as much effort into serving really top-quality coffee as we do in our shops.

Coffee is, even more than usual, the prime focus at outside catering events. Depending on the event, we might bring along some pastries – particularly if there is an early start and people will rely on us for breakfast. But there is not really the possibility of making sandwiches or salads to order. The biggest challenge is usually the rush at certain pinch-points in the day, such as a 20-minute break between shows at Fashion Week, when a large queue will form instantly and we have to be able to make 50 or more cups of coffee in speedy succession – which requires good planning and adequate, experienced staffing.

COFFEE BY THE BAG: RETAIL OPTIONS

Most coffee shops will have some kind of retail offer, as both an extra revenue stream, a service to customers and an added point of interest. At the very least, you will probably want to sell bags of the coffee beans you serve, allowing you to buy in larger quantities – which will endear you to your suppliers and roasters and lower their wholesale prices to you. (You need not worry that this takes away the reason to buy the cup from you: people rarely have the equipment, expertise or patience to brew at home to professional barista standards. They visit your coffee shop for just that, for reasons of convenience and conviviality, and for the little luxury of 'going out'.)

To go with the coffee beans – sold whole or ground, and perhaps also in pods compatible with Nespresso machines – you may also stock coffee-making equipment such as filter papers, Hario V60 coffee drippers, AeroPress models, perhaps some small grinders, plus a selection of jugs, mugs and cups. Depending on your clientele, you may want to go further in this direction, selling more ambitious and expensive equipment, along with a selection of hard-to-find magazines and books devoted to coffee.

Given that most coffee shops operate on a takeaway basis, you are already in effect selling pastries and other bits retail. But, whether you bake yourself or order in, it may not be a good idea to sell a dozen croissants or a whole cake to one customer and have nothing left for regular drop-ins – so you might want to provide this service only on an advance-order basis, which would suit customers planning a birthday cake at home, or a local office organising a Friday coffee-and-pastries meeting in their boardroom.

You can also support specialist suppliers by selling their niche products in your coffee shop: jams, pickles, juices, handmade yoghurt or raw milk, for instance (there seems little point to me in stocking commercially made products that are readily available in supermarkets). And like many coffee and other independent niche shops, we have T-shirts and tote bags bearing our logo.

From this point, the retail offer can be taken as far as you want it, up to and including making your business a true hybrid coffee shop. I know of a vintage vinyl/coffee shop, a comics and manga/coffee shop and several florist/coffee shops or cycle/coffee shops. It depends on your personal interests and contacts, the space you have and your potential clientele. For a while, I shared my first space with a contact who sold niche art magazines, as a way to split the rent and draw a wider audience (for more on this, see chapter 5). Having decided to narrow my focus to coffee and food, I still have a rack of organic cotton T-shirts sourced from a small-scale maker in Lisbon – again, these are items unavailable elsewhere in Copenhagen.

Another avenue worth pursuing to increase footfall and raise awareness is hosting events, possibly after hours or at times of the day when you are usually quiet (it was partly to be able to host this type of event, and to develop the retail side of the business, that I opened a second branch of Darcy's Kaffe in what was clearly going to be a less frantic spot). These can be coffee related: there is enough interest in coffee these days that making or tasting sessions are in demand, and sometimes a company will hire me to give their team a masterclass as part of a team-building office outing. Other events may not be specifically coffee related, although they might like a drink thrown in: book launches; poetry readings; book club meetings; art exhibitions if you have enough wall space for display; lectures; music evenings and recitals.

12 BUSINESS STUDIES

Doing 'the books'; margin vs mark-up; key calculations; independence vs outside investors; common mistakes and how to avoid them.

We've left it till last but, sorry, there's no escaping the reality that we have to confront the innocent-sounding but dreaded 'books'. I didn't open a coffee shop for the paperwork – after all, it was my escape from the desk job that landed me here in the first place. And I'm happy to admit that this is not my strongest suit. My nearest and dearest nagged me for months to do a crash course in business but I was always too busy actually *doing* the business... well, that was my excuse to myself. Perhaps it just wasn't me.

But I have managed to pick up a few tips along the way, partly through the school of hard knocks, and I hope that running through some of them here will make it easier for you to avoid some of the pitfalls that lie in wait. You might be coming at this from a different angle from me (hopeless romantic humanities student with a burning passion for coffee and people) and you might already be fluent in the language of business; if this is the case, then I suggest you skip this section and focus your attention on some of the preceding chapters. But if you are staying with me, I'll try to make it as painless (and amusing) as possible – all with the aim of saving you, the budding café owner, from the pain of messing up. Hindsight is a wonderful thing, after all, and you might as well benefit from mine.

The truth of the matter is that I didn't really consider my initial foray into coffee shops a business at all. I didn't go into it necessarily to make money and I didn't take on any investment or loans, so I had no need to present or justify my plans to a third party. From there, things just seemed to snowball.

THE BUSINESS PLAN
Looking back, however, I now believe it is worth having a really good think *before* diving headlong into opening a business, and that you should sketch out some concrete ideas, otherwise known as a business plan.

Speaking honestly, if with a degree of shame, I only put pen to paper (or digit to keyboard) in this fashion a year or so after launching, once I had discovered the wealth of templates and help available on the internet. I would particularly recommend LivePlan.com, a US-based platform that makes it easy to rustle up a solid plan whatever your location (although irritatingly, the default currency is in US dollars and can't be changed; if you need to present the plan to third parties, simply remember to attach a note at the top explaining that you are in fact referring to euros or pounds sterling, or whatever your working currency).

At the thinking and planning stage it seems impossible to predict what will happen when you start, and once you do, the goalposts will probably change immediately and possibly keep doing so week by week, month by month. But believe me, even if you aren't looking to justify your plans to a third party in order to secure funding and even if you are awful with numbers and/or writing and it's the last thing you want to do, getting some kind of plan down on paper will help to clarify your intentions, if to no one other than yourself. It will make it easier to identify glaring errors, for example, in your pricing strategy, or even in your main concept – the numbers may tell you that although you seem to be making a lot of cups of coffee, they're not recording much of a profit; or that although you seem to run out of sandwiches early in the day, they are earning well.

This process will also help to narrow down your choices and potentially make some decisions for you: What equipment should you start with? What kind of location does your concept suit? You will need to stay flexible and open to changes in direction, so if a good opportunity comes along that isn't what you have written down, you can redraw your business plan and see if it still adds up. The LivePlan platform mentioned above makes updating and editing very straightforward, perhaps even pleasurable – and I'm not sure that's a word often used to describe business plan writing. It is also easy to have several plans running concurrently, which can help keep all bases covered.

Of course, a business plan is not just an exercise in self-actualisation. If you want to open a business account with a bank, you will almost certainly need to provide a fairly detailed plan of action. I won't go into the full rundown (plenty of these kinds of resources can be found online), but the main areas of concern will be initial outlay and the funding for that; projected cash flow for the first year; and profit and loss expected in the first year. This section of your plan will need to add up and be realistic. It often pays to add or subtract 20 to 30 per cent to or from your numbers in a pessimistic, worst-case direction (that is, adding to your projected costs to make allowance for unforeseen expenses while subtracting from projected income to stay at the conservative end of estimates) in order to end up with a realistic and achievable plan. It is always good to under-promise and over-deliver – even to yourself. After all, you don't want to look like a hapless contestant on *Dragons' Den* as the shrewd tycoons raise their eyebrows in bemused shock at bold claims of a million-pound business in year two.

BREAKING (EVEN)

One really useful calculation you can do in advance of opening or even selecting a site/concept – one that really provides you with an insight into what *can* work and what is actually feasible – is an analysis of the break-even point. Essentially, you need to add up all the costs of running the shop (rent, energy costs, salaries, cost of goods and so on) and break it down into a daily total. Obviously this changed a lot in my case after the move from the basement to Rantzausgade and the hiring of staff, and it's a figure that will fluctuate dramatically as a business grows and costs change, so the calculation needs to be updated regularly.

If you project that your shop will need to hit, for example, €1,000 a day, or £1,000 a day, to start making a profit, you know that you need to be pretty busy while also making sure your costs (particularly staffing) don't creep up. Break this figure down into the number of cups of coffee that need to be sold. Perhaps it's 300 cups – so a *lot* of coffees! Perhaps your site has the location, footfall and layout to support that. Perhaps you will need to add some other items (pastries, food, retail) to bump up the average spend per head so you can hit that figure with a lower number of customers. Just keep in mind that the more elements you add (food especially), the more staff you will need to do this well, so the higher your break-even point. This may seem like infuriating carousel thinking, but starting to think early on about this stuff will help you find the right balance in your business from the start.

DEALING WITH BANKS & 'THE BOOKS'

The days of trailing up and down the high street, tail between your legs and clutching your business plan, hoping to find a kind face behind the desk at a bank are, thankfully, over. In most countries it is now possible to find a digital solution that can quickly and without too much expense (although business accounts are never exactly cheap) set you up with what you need to start receiving payments and paying bills and salaries. Some will even help you organise your finances in a much more helpful way than a traditional bank.

Most of your communications and business transactions (orders, invoices, taxes, payroll) will be online, so it makes sense to be on the same level. I'm a big fan of what I see as the democratisation of banking, but I guess the one big caveat is that you won't have an adviser to speak to. You probably won't be able to get a loan (some digital banks are offering deals with third-party brokers, but watch out for these – their terms may be onerous) and you won't have access to an overdraft or line of credit. Treat your business account as more of an online wallet where you can hold, organise and shift your business's money around. It's also essential to split what is personal money and what belongs to your business from the outset – don't waste weeks and a small fortune creating this division.

Depending on your skills at keeping abreast of the flow of money – sorting out receipts, keeping on top of invoices both paid and to be paid and so on – you will need some level of assistance. Running a coffee shop doesn't leave you with a lot of free time, and the busier you get, the less time you will find yourself able to devote to doing the books. Even if things aren't overly busy from the outset, it is better to make a start on the right foot and establish a good routine for your paperwork.

It's not absolutely necessary, however, to hire an accountant or book-keeper. There are some useful online resources that will help you organise this side of the business for a small monthly subscription, and for most countries they will be tailored to your local tax rules and regulations. One of these, QuickBooks, will make it possible to create and send invoices, structure your income and outgoings and prepare reports to keep an eye on profit/loss, cost of goods and more. An app called Dinero that I started with in Copenhagen will prepare your VAT return and give you a step-by-step on how to submit it yourself for an extra fee.

An accountant might be necessary to report your annual tax return, though, so it is worth finding one in your network who you feel will do a good job – I would always want a personal recommendation for an accountant. Make sure they are fully registered to report tax. As your business grows and your time shrinks, the sheer numbers may increase beyond the levels you feel comfortable with handling by yourself, so it may well be an idea to find an accountant or bookkeeper to help you keep on top of things. Try to find somebody you can meet with in person or at least via Zoom. Sitting down with a specialist who can explain the intricacies of tax systems is invaluable, and they may well suggest areas where you can save money or allowances you did not know you could claim. They might also be useful to spar with, bouncing off ideas about spending, saving, future investment and so on.

One tip I picked up through my own ignorance and mistakes is to have separate accounts set up within your overall business account. If you lump everything together, you are in danger of losing track of how much you need to keep aside to make certain payments, which means you can be blindsided by a surprise bill. Most banks will allow you – possibly for a small charge, but I would argue that it will save you money in the long run – to open multiple sub-accounts which you can designate according to what you need: one for VAT, one for salaries, one for rent/expenses/invoices/loan payments and so on.

When you receive payments from your point of sale (POS) (which can usually be set to daily, weekly or monthly), you can work out how much of this amount consists of VAT (usually the POS will show you). You then simply transfer this amount to the VAT account and don't touch it until you need to file your VAT returns. In the same way, you can designate a certain percentage of the takings to move into the other accounts, leaving you in good shape to pay your big bills and hopefully enough to cover all the other day-to-day expenses and invoices. Working in this way will also give you a pretty good up-to-date impression of the financial health of your business. If there is not enough money coming in to split into these sub-accounts, or you find yourself having to dip into them too often, there is potentially a problem somewhere that needs to be looked at, at least when it comes to cash flow.

PRICING

Putting prices on the menu is one of the trickiest tasks in any coffee shop. It's a good idea to get the pricing right from the start because it can be difficult to make early changes with a new customer base if you realise too late that you've made some miscalculations.

When I started slinging coffee in the basement, I wanted above all to be accessible. I didn't want to be the new expensive coffee shop that was only meant for certain kinds of people. The location definitely had some part to play in this, as I was on the rougher end of a street in a very mixed area. I didn't want to ruffle feathers and be branded 'hipster', 'snobby', 'pretentious' or 'overpriced'. My clear success in this intention was brought home by an early (and gratifying) review in a national newspaper under a headline that translated more or less as 'Copenhagen's cosiest homeless shelter'. While I took this as a slightly backhanded compliment, we didn't have the budget to spiff up the interiors all that much and our pricing was very much at the affordable end considering the quality of the products I was serving.

When we moved into our new location on Rantzausgade, the level of investment and the outgoings each month were considerably higher and finally I had to hire a team so there were salaries to be paid. All of these factors meant I needed to raise the prices; the change in situation demanded it.

The Margin

Broadly speaking, with a coffee shop you are in the business of adding value to relatively inexpensive raw materials, which means the mark-up can look pretty appealing from the proprietor's point of view. But as I have written earlier, each transaction is pretty small so you have to sell a lot of cups of coffee to make a decent profit.

There are two ways of looking at prices – two perspectives, if you like: that of the business and that of the customer. Ideally, you should keep both in mind and your prices should look reasonable from both perspectives.

As a business, you need to figure out what your profit margin needs to be on any given product. Industry norms are that gross margins on coffee should lie somewhere between 70 to 80 per cent. This might sound like a licence to print money but in fact it is simply the margin on top of the raw materials – the coffee and milk – and does not include all the other costs involved in being open for the day. For food prepared on site, the standard margin is a little lower at around 70 per cent, and you should aim for a 30 to 40 per cent margin on products bought in from elsewhere.

Before you get excited about how profitable your business could be and start wondering why *everyone* doesn't do this for a living, you need to think about two things. Firstly, your *net* profit, which is essentially all the costs involved in operating the business that chip away at every coffee you sell. To help illustrate just how brutal this can be on that pot of gold you thought you had waiting for you at the end of the gross margin rainbow, let's look at a breakdown of costs on an average day at the Rantzausgade Darcy's Kaffe to show the net profit.

WEDNESDAY 16 NOVEMBER 2022

	€
Revenue (without sales tax)	**2125.24**
Cost of goods	756.00
Salaries[6]	1026.51
Rent & facilities	144.42
Administrative costs	98.25
Operating expenses	16.11
Total expenses	2041.29
Net profit	**83.95**

This average day in the winter gives a small return of just under four per cent profit overall. This shows just how small the gains can be – despite a decent day with around 200 coffees sold and a decent lunch rush. Yes, it can get busier than this and when the weather is better we can do more covers with people sitting outside. But then if we get much busier, our costs also go up as staff need to work longer shifts or we have an extra member of the team on the floor.

The second key thing to think about when making these plans and calculations is factoring in that bad day that comes along every once in a while without warning (usually connected to the weather or in our case with an overly active Copenhagen municipality road maintenance department). Or perhaps you won't hit the ground running with your projected sales – it may take time to build the number of cups sold per day. If you don't consider these possibilities – more like probabilities – in your forecasting, it will come as a nasty shock when you see yourself going into

---

6 Including management and back office.

the red. As has been mentioned earlier, it's best to start off cautiously and pessimistically (in your calculations and spending – not your attitude or demeanour) and then build from there.

CALCULATING PRICE

Once you've started to think about these scenarios, you can start to try to formulate your prices. Take the cost of the raw materials involved (so in the case of a flat white: the espresso, the milk or equivalent, the cup and lid if it's a takeaway), plus the cost of labour, rent, electricity, tax and so on, and add the standard profit margin of around 80 per cent to that figure.

If the calculation results in a number that you think represents (more than) good value for the quality of product, of service and experience, and you think it stacks up favourably to the local competition, then be confident and charge a little more. After all, this calculation represents the *minimum* you need to charge to cover all the costs in the business (and there may well be hidden costs you have failed to include). Remember, the aim is to try to make a little actual profit, if only to reinvest in the business or provide a buffer to tide you over in an emergency.

Now, think about that price from the point of view of a customer. I like to go back to my basic premise from Chapter 1 that a visit to a coffee shop falls somewhere between a necessity – an essential service – and an affordable little luxury. It should be accessible to more or less everybody: we're not operating a charity, but students and anybody with a wage should be able to drop in regularly, not just for a birthday treat.

Before setting any prices it is worth spending a day surveying the coffee shops within a decent radius and noting down the prices of various coffees, pastries, banana bread and sandwiches. When I do this (and I repeat the exercise every couple of months), a pretty clear picture soon emerges of the sweet spot that I can charge for each item without raising any hackles at the expense on the one hand or looking cheap on the other. With any luck, the prices I have calculated from the business perspective will fall somewhere in this sweet spot. If not – if my calculated prices look too expensive – perhaps I need to look again at my costs (are the ingredients just too expensive for this market? Are my staffing costs too high?) or even at my whole concept.

If I do manage to charge prices that are close enough to the average in my area, that means I am not competing with my rivals on price, which can only end up as a race to the bottom – and frankly, I'm not really interested in customers whose main motivation is to buy the cheapest cup of coffee in town. I also know that customers will see my café as somehow 'price neutral' – neither particularly cheap nor expensive – which frees them up (or forces them) to judge us on what really matters: the quality of the coffee, food and service they receive, and the overall vibe of their visit.

So now we are back on the territory I prefer: how can I give my customers an improved experience, a better cup of coffee, tastier snacks and meals? Instead of compromising down, of thinking like a corporate chain, in terms of profit per unit, I am thinking like a host. This to me is the essence of hospitality and the challenge I want to take up – to pour a cup of coffee I can be proud of, and offer pastries and sandwiches you won't find anywhere else.

It is far more interesting to me to scour the world's roasters and cultivate my contacts in the industry to find special coffees that I can share with my customers than it is to hunt around for the cheapest deal on avocados or whatever. By and large, I am usually happy to pay the standard rates to speciality suppliers of coffee and produce, whom I regard as my partners in trade.

I do try to keep the price of even the rarest, most exotic coffee close to the local standard. A market does exist for really expensive coffees costing £20 or more a shot (or its equivalent in other currencies), but perhaps it is limited to the ritzy quarters of London or Paris, where a certain sort of punter is actively looking to drop big bucks. Just out of interest I once sampled a £25 cup of Panama geisha at one such coffee house in London's Mayfair and was frankly shocked by the ignorance and lack of coffee-making skill displayed by the barista on duty. (I'm not sure how fresh it was, either, given how few they apparently serve.)

There are limits to the price it is worth paying for certain ingredients. For a while I sourced some ultra-high-welfare organic milk which cost nearly as much as reasonable-quality wine per bottle, but a couple of substandard deliveries led me to doubt the company's attention to detail, so I reverted to a more standard organic milk.

There are of course areas where a hard-headed business approach can help cut costs and make savings, such as striking better deals for bulk items such as paper towels or cleaning products.

RAISING PRICES

You might feel you have got your pricing right, but the level will only last for a snapshot of time. We live in an era of rising prices and nobody is immune: the cost of green arabica coffee beans doubled on international markets in the 24 months to July 2022, and staff have the right to expect their wages to keep up with inflation. You will have to raise your prices on a regular basis, just to keep standing still.

Most customers understand the process, so it should not be a problem. But it is well worth giving serious thought to the psychological effects of price rises – and how to minimise negative reactions.

There are two approaches at either end of the spectrum that I think should be avoided if at all possible: what I think of as the 'blunderbuss' approach of calculating a blanket price hike every six months or so that you impose across the menu as a percentage rise. This can annoy the customer for two reasons: everything goes up in price, which can be a shock; and a flat percentage calculation can result in some pretty silly prices (a latte for €3.76 [£3.27] or a sandwich for €7.13 [£6.19]) that smack of a big chain, whose prices are set centrally in an office far away, or of government charges.

At the other end of the spectrum, there are menus that see tiny incremental increases every time you visit – 10 pence on an espresso one day, 20 pence on a bowl of porridge the next – as if the proprietor is trying to smuggle them past you.

My preferred solution is to hold prices at a particular level for as long as you can, then introduce a raft of changes that you believe you can live with for another good period. Try to be as transparent as possible with your customers – especially the regulars you rely on, who will have become accustomed to particular prices – keeping them in the loop via your social media posts, or with clear messaging on your menus. Instead of a blanket increase, focus the main jumps on specific items where they are justified and try to hold other prices steady. Prices should also move up in sensible steps – where possible, units of 5 or 10 – with particular caution paid to crossing the big psychological boundaries: a €10.50 sandwich can look very expensive to a customer who is used to paying €9.

DISCOUNTS

This is potentially a tricky subject, so it is a good idea to think things through before you start slinging your first flat whites across the counter for no charge and find yourself in a bit of a trap. As I've said before, it's more than likely that most of your early custom will be from people who you know personally – friends, family, those who have helped you get set up, and others in the neighbourhood who want to support a new business. Depending on where you are based, the pool of potential customers for a new coffee shop might even be quite small and close to home. And it might well feel a bit strange to be taking good money from people who you normally split rounds with at the pub and exchange small favours with. But look at it this way: most of these people are frequenting your shop not because they want a free coffee but to support someone they know in their new venture, so by giving them free or heavily discounted food or drinks you are actually depriving them of this. They may even stop dropping in because they don't want to feel they are taking advantage of your generosity or sense of obligation.

A case might be made for discounting (or offering complimentary drinks) immediately after your new coffee shop opens, in order to bring some action to a potentially quiet site and draw attention to something new in the area. But if you are going to apply this logic, just be careful how long this period goes on for – you don't want to annoy friends when prices they have got used to suddenly leap up. And where do you draw the line? At some point, most regular customers end up being friends, so who deserves the discount and who doesn't? When you start to hire staff who might be taking payments from people they don't know well, do you really want to have to go over each time and explain in a hushed voice what kind of discount this particular customer receives? It begins to get a little complicated very quickly.

One way of handling this issue is to invite your friends to an opening-day party where everything is free – coffee, bites, a few bottles with alcohol later on. You could also have a so-called 'soft opening' for a clearly defined period such as a week, with a 30 per cent discount on all bills. As to looking after those regulars who graduate to being personal friends, I have already suggested (Chapter 8, page 113) that you could invite them along to your anniversary after-hours celebrations, with drinks and nibbles on the house.

Another approach I much prefer when people I know well come to the café (so-called VIP customers) is to offer them a taste of a new pastry we are developing, or a sample of a new coffee we are dialling in. I try to be a bit subtle about it so the customers sitting on the neighbouring tables don't feel left out (maybe I'll even give them a sample too if they look curious). So I do feel that certain people who are super-close to the café, or have done some work for us in the past, deserve to have a little special treatment sometimes – just not free/discounted drinks from the menu. This very much depends on me or one of my more experienced managers being on duty – new staff who don't know the faces will not be able to carry out the same service (at least at the beginning), but I don't think this would really worry any of my friends.

The one exception to all this is delivery people. I will always offer someone who has dropped off something for us nicely a free drink, whether that be a DHL person with a consignment of coffee boxes or our lovely kombucha supplier, Table Ferments, who bring their bottles themselves by bike every week. This is just a nice little thank-you for their work and normally ensures they will prioritise us next time and ensure we get deliveries promptly and safely. Other coffee shops might extend the same courtesy to local police and other services – a small gesture that also potentially benefits the business through extra surveillance.

As for ongoing discounts to reward the loyalty of regulars, see the box on 'The Book' on page 111.

THE BREAKDOWN

One approach to planning your business while scouting for locations and considering different concepts is to portion out what you will spend your money on, and frame that against what you think you can make at the site – that is, your projected takings. There are a couple of simple rules of thumb that might help you make a decision on whether a particular site or concept can work, or whether the site might require a different approach to succeed.

First of all, the rent. It is a good start if you can project that the rental for the month can be earned in a single day of business, or two at a push. If you feel this will be a stretch with what you can envisage taking in a day, perhaps the rent is just too high for the concept you have in mind.

Similarly, there is the issue of staff costs. In the beginning, perhaps you as the owner will take the brunt of the hours on the bar, as I did for the first three years or so of the business. Even once you pay yourself a salary, you are not going to bump it up to cover all the hours you work. But as you start to take a back seat from frontline shifts, as you almost certainly will in the longer term – or even if you have no intention of withdrawing altogether at any point, which I would not advise – then you need to keep a close eye on staff costs in relation to your turnover.

Every shop is a little different, depending on factors such as whether you offer food that requires serious prep or whether you offer table service, but if over the week staff pay averages in excess of 40 per cent of your revenue, then your business is really going to struggle. On the flipside, if staff costs fall below 25 per cent of your revenue, you are really going to be pushing your team hard and the chances are that service, quality and customer experience will almost certainly suffer – not to mention the morale of your belea-guered team, who may well decide not to stick around.

At Darcy's Kaffe, we often reach the 40 per cent mark during slower weekdays, but we use these relatively high-cost days to prep for the busier days at the end of the week, when costs tend to dip below 30 per cent – so we average out at a manageable number overall. But this is something you need to keep a vigilant eye on as the numbers can fluctuate constantly due to factors including the weather, public and school holidays, and the infamous payday rush. Some advanced scheduling software can give you a day-to-day reading of this number, but if you are doing your own calculation, remember to use the figure for your takings *minus* the addition of sales tax otherwise it will give you a very misleading picture.

So the equation here is:

Salaries (including extras)/NET sales turnover x 100 = staff costs in %

There's another calculation that can't be measured numerically, but is equally important:

As your highest cost, staff are your biggest investment – but if you establish the right culture (see page 122), also poten-tially your biggest asset

'INVISIBLE BUT ESSENTIAL' COSTS
Insurance & Liabilities

You really must look into the legal requirements for insurance in your area of operation before you get started. This can take a moment or two to sort out because you'll need to compare quotes from different providers; price comparison websites such as MoneySavingExpert.com and its equivalents will help you with this. You'll also need to show the insurance people your space and provide them with information on how much the equipment and furniture are worth, along with your expected earnings and stock levels.

Remember, this is all to protect you in the case of the unthinkable: fire, water, criminal damage and so on – the shop front next door to Darcy's Kaffe on Rantzausgade was destroyed when a car drove into it, a reminder that anything can happen. So make sure you are not going to get caught short when it comes to making a claim.

Even if you are running a mobile coffee cart or something similar and you don't have a physical space or storage to protect, you'll need some kind of public liability insurance in case a customer gets sick as a result of something you have served them.

All these invisible, boring but essential costs need to be taken into consideration when calculating your start-up finances.

THREE KEY MISTAKES I MADE
Pricing Too Low

In the very beginning, my aim was to serve the best of the best, for a price that nobody could argue with. I was also sufficiently self-aware to realise that my set-up was far from professional and sleek and I felt my prices should reflect that.

All true to some extent, but if I had kept my prices low I would never have been able to change the set-up for the better – there would never have been a surplus to reinvest.

I also learnt there are other factors that are as important as prices when gaining acceptance in a community. Being friendly and engaged with those around the shop and those who dropped in attracted a base of regulars who wanted to support us – and not just for the great prices. You're creating value in another way.

Of course, you need to respect your community: it may not be a good idea to offer a slice of cake you have to sell for the price of most people's lunch. But remember that good value does not mean cheap (and vice versa).

Too Many Bar Hours, Not Enough Business Hours

In the early days of Darcy's Kaffe, if we were open, I was behind the bar – I had no staff, so there was no alternative. But if you work too many hours on the floor or on the bar, the paperwork quickly piles up and you're left with a mess to deal with on your days/hours off. I tried to dedicate one good session a week to respond to emails, check invoices and so on. It wasn't nearly enough!

Pennies Make Pounds

One knock-on effect of being so tied up on the bar was that I was always living in the moment, obsessed with getting through the day with as many small wins as possible (serving the best coffees, having great chats with people, building up relationships with new regulars, keeping the place spick and span).

This might sound ideal. But it was hard to take a step back and focus on the bigger picture – there was no perspective to my planning. So when it came to seemingly small decisions, I would always go with my gut – which butter to use (the best, obviously), which milk to go with as a standard (same answer as before, obviously). These small items of lavish expenditure didn't faze me. We were trying to be the best, after all.

But small expenses, combined with the regular trickle of price increases across the board, do add up (and eat into your profit margin). They *seem* imperceptible when you view them from the day-to-day perspective I was stuck in, but as soon as you extrapolate them to a monthly or yearly increase, you recognise the true scale of the sums involved.

As it has been said elsewhere, raindrops make oceans. How many litres of milk do you get through a year? How many napkins? I'm certainly not advocating the cheap solution at all times – but you must make the effort to make informed decisions on your costs.

POTENTIAL MISTAKES I MANAGED TO AVOID
Going Big – Going Home

While I have definitely made my share of mistakes since launching Darcy's Kaffe, there are a few big ones that I'm glad I avoided. Some of these were more a matter of pure luck and circumstance than savvy business instinct, but still. The first that springs to mind, and it's something that you see all the time, is the coffee shop that opens with a bang and a lot of glitz, but struggles and then closes with a whimper. These are often sites that have undergone a massive refit, involving high-end lighting, glossy surfaces and costly equipment, and perhaps assumed they would be busy from day one. Maybe the operators actually did a business plan with a proper forecast before borrowing/spending what seemed like a good investment. Maybe not. Numbers or no numbers, I would always recommend veering on the side of caution and not blowing the budget before you have the cash flow to back it up. Better to keep some cash in reserve to act as a buffer in the case of a slow start (three months of salary and rent costs would be great), see how the opening period goes, and then make informed decisions about how to add further shine to the space.

As you will have gathered if you have reached this far in the book, I have always been ambitious to achieve the highest standards of coffee and service and I have tried to avoid cutting corners – which so often ends up with cutting standards. One mistake that coffee shop operators around the world often make is over-reliance on cheap, young and inexperienced staff. Of course it is important to recruit new staff into the industry, but they are only effective if they are working alongside experienced mentors and managers who lead them by example. It is unreasonable to expect them to guess the best or quickest way to do something: put simply, they will do it badly.

Yes, you make a saving on salaries – but this comes at a cost to your business, sometimes an immediate one. One hot day last summer I was strolling with a friend beside the Serpentine lake in London's Hyde Park, a part of town always busy with tourists, when we decided to stop for a coffee at a permanent outdoor stall. There was a fairly long queue, as might have been expected, but after 10 minutes or so it hadn't moved, so I wandered up to the front to investigate. There I discovered that the stall was being run by a couple of girls in their mid-teens – quite possibly the children of the stallholder, earning pocket money in their school holidays – and they quite clearly could not cope with the volume of trade. We walked off to find a coffee elsewhere, and I'm sure plenty of others did the same. A good, experienced barista working with one or both of these young assistants would have sold twice as many coffees throughout the day.

INDEPENDENCE VS OUTSIDE INVESTMENT

This book is not a business primer. It makes no attempt to tell you how to structure your enterprise in light of taxation, personal liability and other legal requirements (which anyway will vary depending on your local jurisdiction). For information and advice on these matters, you should consult other books (there are literally thousands of business books to choose between) and/or seek professional legal and financial assistance. But I do have some advice to pass on from experience that might help you address some important questions around financing and outside investment.

As you'll have read earlier, I'm happy that I didn't take on unnecessary outside investment or partners for the launch of Darcy's Kaffe. Starting off on a modest scale, I was able to bootstrap the entire operation and put all proceeds beyond my basic living expenses back into the business – and the tiny budgets I worked with were very effective in keeping me disciplined. It might not be a perfect way for everyone as progress was slow in the beginning, but it meant that I was able to run with my vision without having to compromise or convince anybody else. I'm not oblivious to the fact that my situation was pretty unique, given the favourable property situation in Copenhagen and having a supportive and talented architect in my life. If your circumstances are different and the barriers to entry are higher (in a high-rent city, perhaps), then it may be that you have to secure capital in advance. I would just say be careful about who you take money from and the terms that might bring. Borrowing money from family might be the best option, taking a loan from the bank might be the next best, while partnering with someone and giving some of the company away might actually be the worst idea.

This does not mean that all outside investment is permanently taboo. At certain stages of growth, a cash injection may be necessary. For instance, opening a second venue might mean doubling your overheads overnight – which is difficult to achieve on the back of organic growth alone. So it might be necessary to seek investment from one source or another to make a leap in scale.

Another potential turning point is when you take on the responsibilities that come with employing staff on a permanent basis. In the early days of Darcy's Kaffe, when I was working solo, I hoped to 'earn' enough in two or three days' takings to pay the rent for the month. That meant I was essentially covered as a business. An emergency that closed the shop for a day, a week or even more – a flood, a fire, a power failure or (as it turned out) a pandemic – could be taken in my stride: I would simply be strapped for cash personally for a few days. Once you have half a dozen salaries to cover in the absence of any income, the situation is very different: you will be in trouble as a business within a matter of days if you have no cash reserves.

An outside investor can also bring all sorts of advantages in terms of business know-how and contacts. They will probably be more experienced than you and possess different skills, and can scrutinise your operation using the head as well as the heart – offering the perspective you lack because you've simply been too close to the project from day one: it's your baby, after all, the apple of your eye.

At the time of writing, for both these above-mentioned reasons, I am considering taking on investment for the first time. My potential partners are a marketing specialist who has built and sold his own company and a serial investor who is brilliant at the nuts and bolts of deal-making and negotiation. Both will be on hand to advise me and spar with me on subjects that are pretty much beyond my comprehension, or at least my experience. Most importantly, they see eye to eye with me on the principles of Darcy's Kaffe and how to progress from the point we have now reached. Brian, the marketing guru, is a regular customer who fell in love with the original basement café in its infancy and has been pretty much a daily visitor ever since. I am confident they are the right investors for me. Check back in the second edition to see how it goes. ☺

7 DAYS TO OPENING:
THE COUNTDOWN

This countdown assumes that you have read this book, absorbed its contents and decided what sort of coffee shop you want. In other words you should have thought carefully about your coffee and food menus and about interior design – the potential look of your shop and begun to assemble what you need to create that effect – furniture furniture, light fittings and equipment – over the previous months. If you try to buy it all in a hurry, it will almost certainly cost you more, but look cheap.

First, a checklist of advance preparations:
- Make sure you have coffee already in stock and 'resting' ready for the opening!
- Pre-buy as much as possible – furniture, soft furnishings, light fittings, plants, equipment, coffee. Then the week you move in to the space you won't need to wait around for deliveries or hunt around town and your coffee will be resting, ready for opening.
- Make sure your basic furniture, fittings and coffee-making/kitchen equipment are all in good repair, clean and functional.
- Carry out a thorough **site inspection**: floors, walls, services (plumbing and electrics). TAKE PHOTOS (+ videos) to show builders and other contractors. If possible, bring them along to your site inspection so there are no nasty surprises when you get the keys.
- Line up and book any **tradespeople** you may need (plumber, specialist water company, electrician, decorator, plasterer, carpenter and so on) so they are ready to move in on Day One.
- **Plan** the space as much as you can – the central bar is the most important element and will act as a focal point, even if there are other things that are not yet complete when you first open.

- Construct any fitted furniture off-site and in advance. Then you can simply move the pieces in, put them in position and fix them down, if door or window dimensions permit.
- Start off with Instagram and other platforms as soon as you have a brand/direction. You don't even need a physical space already secured to start building up a little hype around the coffee shop. But be careful what you post about and how much detail you give until all is confirmed. Don't over-promise – a little mystery only adds to the allure.

DAY ONE

Collect keys and inspect site.

Make an immediate start on any messy structural work required to ensure electricity/plumbing/lighting is functional.

If the floor needs attention, ditto.

Working around the above, carpenter to begin assembling shelves/bar and installing fitted units which have been assembled off-site.

Clean (and if necessary strip/fill) walls to prepare for painting.

Black out windows with posters advertising the opening.

Make a start on any external changes needed: at minimum, clean/strip the facade for painting and signage. Attach any hanging signage as soon as possible to attract attention from passers-by – a chalkboard on the pavement can shout 'OPEN SOON' with a seven-day countdown.

Continue online campaign, with a new 'teaser' story/pic on Instagram every day to opening.

DAY TWO

Paint undercoat on all walls.

(Note: it may be a good idea to do most of the painting in the evening/ overnight when plumber/electrician/carpenter have gone, to avoid getting in each other's way. If you are decorating yourself or with friends, this work can be done pretty quickly unless your space is cavernous.)

DAY THREE

Start moving in furniture and equipment, keeping it covered with dust sheets to avoid paint damage.

Begin painting, starting with the ceiling.

DAY FOUR

Aim to have the main structure in place – service bar, till, sinks, coffee machines etc.

You might need to get in an espresso machine technician and/or plumber to help install piping etc.

DAY FIVE

Run tests on all equipment.

Dial in coffees and see how they are tasting. Hopefully you have enough rested coffee ready for the hordes of customers you hope to be serving.

DAY SIX

Make final touches to decoration/signage etc – there will be bits of painting that can't be finalised until everything is in place. Painting smaller things can always come later though – in the meantime, use soft furnishings to hide/disguise.

Bring in all your crockery and cutlery, polished to a sparkle.

Make sure everything you need is stocked, including retail shelves.

Run through your processes to ensure everything is working to order. Think of it as a dress rehearsal for a play.

DAY SEVEN

Put fresh flowers in vases. dust surfaces and polish equipment.

Invite friends/family/contacts/neighbours for the opening day jamboree and make sure you commission a decent photographer to take some nice photos you can share afterwards. Make sure your Instagram account and relevant hashtags are properly set up and visible so people can tag you.

And remember: the coffee shop does not have to be perfect from Day One. With the best possible preparations, there will inevitably be things you want to tweak and improvements you want to make, whether overnight in the first few days or over a day or two when you're closed a few months in.

Where you can – and certainly should – strive for perfection from the moment you hang the 'open' sign on your door is in your attitude and hospitality. Every customer who crosses your threshold should be made to feel welcome and be served the best possible cup of coffee and the tastiest plates of food you can make. If you succeed in these aims, you'll easily be forgiven the odd patch of unpainted plaster or occasional opening-month blip.

Above all, have a good time running your coffee shop: make it fun, for yourself, your staff and your customers. Yes, it is work – sometimes extremely hard work. You are now running a business that imposes demands and responsibilities. So try to remember what brought you here in the first place, whether it was a love of coffee, a distaste for office life or a desire to be your own boss. You chose this path and it is up to you to enjoy it as much as you can – and the more you succeed in this, the happier your customers will be.

GLOSSARY

Roasting level (dark vs light)
Refers to the development of the roast. More traditional, Italian espresso is roasted for longer and results in a darker coffee bean with a more bitter, dark-chocolate sweetness. Lighter roasts, often dubbed the Scandinavian style, are distinctively a lighter shade of brown and will taste more mellow and smooth (actual flavour will depend on origin and variety of course). Omni roasting is a style that aims to find a sweet spot in the coffee that will lend it to both espresso and filter brewing. Traditionally, espresso roasts are more developed (darker) than filter roasts.

Panamanian geisha
Considered one of the 'holy grail' coffees, geisha is one of the most highly sought after varieties of coffee bean. It was first commercially propagated by coffee farms in Panama. There are a number of very well equipped (and wealthy) coffee producers in Panama who have the resources to invest in these high-value crops which they can sell for extremely high prices relative to other coffee varieties.

Basket
The small metal basket, perforated with lots of tiny holes that allow coffee to flow through, which holds the coffee.

VST
A specific brand of basket manufactured to ensure the holes are even and consistent – not always true of others, especially espresso machine company defaults.

Portafilter
The coffee 'arm' which holds the basket into which the ground coffee goes before being placed into the espresso machine.

Tamper

Tool used to flatten and compress the ground coffee into a compact and even puck which is ready to be inserted into the coffee machine to be brewed.

Hand brew

FIlter coffee produced by hand rather than a machine. Slower and more delicate than a batch brewer but usually only suitable for one or two cups at a time.

RO

Reverse Osmosis water filter. Essentially this machine uses a semi-permeable membrane to strip the tap water down to a zero state, getting rid of the 'bad water', and then builds it back up to be at preferred level to be used for coffee-making.

PPM

Parts per million. In the context of water, we're measuring the total amount of dissolved minerals in the water – around 50–100 is optimal, although it depends on who you ask. Some might want a lower level for filter coffee and a higher one for espresso.

Groups

Refers to the group head of an espresso machine, from which the espresso emerges. A one-group machine is usually a domestic size, two groups is standard commercial size, three and upwards is considered large. Proud Mary in Melbourne is infamous for its six-group Synesso machine while Rosslyn in London has one three-group machine next to a two-group model.

Backflush

In order to keep your espresso machine clean during service, and as part of the daily post-service deep clean, insert the 'blind' basket (the one with no holes) into the portafilter and run a couple of shots on each group of the machine. You will probably see a little coffee in the basket each time. This is what you don't want lingering in the machine. See online resources for more on this.

Our equipment set-up at time of writing

Espresso machine
La Marzocco PB 3-group

Grinders
MahlKönig E65S GBW
Nuova Simonelli Mythos One
MahlKönig EK43

Tamper
PUQpress Q2

Batch brewer
Fetco CBS-2131 XTS, with Litmus Coffee Lab UFO spray-head attachment

Hand brews
Hario V60 2 – plastic model with Hario 2 papers
Bonavita kettle

Water filtration
Pentair Everpure Conserv 75E Reverse Osmosis System – with added storage tank

Milk pitchers
Barista Hustle and others

Scales
Felicita Parallel and Arc models

RESOURCES

Online Resources
Sprudge
Sca
Keys to the Shop (podcast)
Cat and Cloud (podcast)
Barista Hustle
Home Barista

Hand brewers
www.nytimes.com/wirecutter/
reviews/gear-for-making-great-coffee/
www.seriouseats.com/best-pourov-
er-coffee-makers-5441631

Processing
christopherferan.
com/2022/08/19/a-sort-of-glossary-
of-coffee-processes/
coffeechronicler.com/washed-natu-
ral-honey-processing/

Machine cleaning
espressoschool.com.au/blog/
cleaning-coffee-machine

Platforms and apps
RatioCalc app
Liveplan.com
omnicalculator.com

YouTube, specifically the channels of
James Hoffman
Lance Hendrick
Emilee Bryant
Seven Seeds coffee roasters
Patrik Rolf – Coffee with April
European Coffee Trip
Tim Wendleboe
Chris Baca (RealChrisBaca)

Books and magazines
Water for Coffee (Maxwell
Colonna-Dashwood)
Coffee Dictionary (Maxwell
Colonna-Dashwood)
The Coffee Atlas, James Hoffman
*What I Know About Running Coffee
Shops*, Colin Harmon
From Nerd To Pro, Patrik Rolf
Unreasonable Hospitality, Will
Guidara
This Is Your Mind on Plants,
Michael Pollan
Let My People Go Surfing, Yves
Chounard
Courier magazine
Solo magazine
Standart magazine

INDEX